WHATEVER
BECAME
OF . . . ?

WHATEVER BECAME OF...?

by
RICHARD LAMPARSKI

Introduction by
CLEVELAND AMORY

CROWN PUBLISHERS, INC., NEW YORK

Acknowledgments

The author would like to express thanks to the following people who helped in the preparation of this book: Eric Benson, William K. Everson, Bob B. Frederick, Robert Ginsberg, Peter Hanson, Don Koll, Dick Lynch, Alfred Monaco, John Robbins, Romano Tozzi, and John Virzi.

The photographs contained in this book are from the author's own collection, were kindly supplied by the personalities themselves, and are part of the collections of: Peter Hanson, John Robbins, John Virzi, and Francis Young.

PRINTED IN THE UNITED STATES OF AMERICA
Tenth Printing, August, 1974

This book of nostalgia is dedicated to the best remembered and most greatly missed lady in my life, my maternal grandmother: Ellen Downey, 1867–1945.

CONTENTS

In Alphabetical Order

INTRODUCTION
by Cleveland Amory

The word "celebrity" is far older than we are inclined to think it is. Once upon a time, it is true, a person might have been said to *have* "celebrity," or fame, but it would have been as meaningless to say "a celebrity" as it would, nowadays, to say "a fame."

But that was a very long time ago—in fact, America's first generally recognized celebrity was John Jacob Astor I. Indeed, as far back as 1836, the *American Quarterly Review,* speaking of Mr. Astor, said, "From an obscure stranger he has made himself one of the 'celebrities' of the country."

In those days, however, the word was still used with quotation marks. But, as far back as mid-century, in 1856, we find no less "a celebrity" than Emerson himself using the word, and without quotation marks, in *English Traits.*

One thing is certain. Although fame itself was once defined by Nicolas Chamfort, the great French wit, as "the advantage of being known to those who do not know us," the fact is that some celebrities at least—as this book amply demonstrates—are remarkably enduring, if not always endearing, people.

In this book, for example, you will find the answers to dozens of your questions about "whatever happened to"—and, more often than not, you will be amazed to find that even if the celebrity no longer has M. Chamfort's "advantage," he or she has substituted for this advantage something that, for them, may well be, in the long run, far more advantageous.

There are, of course, all kinds of celebrities. The star of a TV series this year may well be, in another year, a "has-been," two years from now a "was," and three years from now not known at all. "The world," the English critic John Collins said, "like an accomplished hostess, pays most attention to those whom it will soon forget."

Mr. Collins' words, translated to modern show business terms, become the textbook story:

    (1) Who is Hugh O'Brian?
    (2) Get me Hugh O'Brian.
    (3) Get me a Hugh O'Brian type.
    (4) Get me a young Hugh O'Brian.
    (5) Who is Hugh O'Brian?

Just how ridiculous the whole question of fame can be was illustrated when a columnist in World War II took a poll to find the "world's favorite personality."

The Pope (Pius XII) finished behind Bing Crosby and Frank Sinatra. Others, in order, were Eisenhower, Father Flanagan, MacArthur, Walter Winchell, Sister Kenny, and Bob Hope. Joseph Stalin finished fifteenth.

Once more, translated to modern show business terms, the story becomes that of Kim Novak arriving in Paris and being driven by a chauffeur who proudly informed her that he'd had many other celebrities in his cab. "I have driven Gloria Swanson," said he, "and Cary Grant and President Coty. I have even driven *your President.*"

"What!" exclaimed Miss Novak delightedly. "Harry Cohn!"

But this is one type of celebrity only. There is a second type—as again this book so amply proves—whose names will ring a bell as long as they live, even if we don't know what they are now doing, or even where they are.

And then, too, there is a third and final kind of celebrity—the celebrity who, literally, never dies.

In this book you will find all three kinds. And, among these three kinds, the author had a wide field to choose from. He has chosen not only wisely but interestingly—and perhaps most important of all—entertainingly.

9

December 27, 1926, his heavyweight crown only three months
old, taken from Dempsey.

GENE TUNNEY

The retelling of World Heavyweight Champ Gene Tunney's story reads like pulp fiction from pre-World War I. He is a Horatio Alger character, a Rover Boy, and Jack Armstrong, all rolled into one. His real name is James Joseph Tunney.

Born in 1897 in Lower Manhattan of Irish-Catholic parents, Gene learned to fight just to exist in his neighborhood. His remarkable good looks made it necessary to fight a little better and far more often than most of the kids. Gene worked for a steamship company for a while before entering the United States Marine Corps during World War I, and in 1919 he won the Light-Heavyweight Championship of the A.E.F. in Paris. Upon his discharge he continued boxing.

After ending Georges Carpentier's career by knocking him out in 1924 he became a leading contender for Jack Dempsey's crown.

As much as the press and public disliked Dempsey, Tunney made him liked by comparison. Dempsey had been called a draft-dodger and a shirker. Tunney, because of his refusal to allow the newspapers to exploit his personal life and by admitting that he read poetry and Shakespeare, was the press's whipping boy. Veteran sports writers such as Westbrook Pegler and Paul Gallico now admit that they sat up nights thinking of angles for articles on the contender to humiliate and infuriate him. He didn't sound or act like any boxer they had known, and they disliked him for it. Years later Gallico said of him, "Tunney was never a natural fighter, born to the sport. On the contrary, he was synthetic, and he acquired the mechanics of his trade through long, bitter hours of practice, trial and error. Pegler and myself took an almost perverse joy in hounding this character. When we should have been cheering him to the echo for the perfection of his profession, we hated him instead for working his deceitful arts upon that hero image of ourselves, caveman Dempsey."

The first encounter between Tunney and Dempsey took place on September 23, 1926, at the Sesquicentennial Stadium in Philadelphia. The odds were 4 to 1 on the Champion. Over 120,000 fans paid $1,895,733 to see an upset, after 10 rounds.

Their second meeting still holds the record for the largest gate in the history of boxing—$2,658,600. It was held in Soldiers Field, Chicago, one year and four days after the first match. Tunney was ahead on points until the seventh round. Then all at once Dempsey let loose and Gene was down for the first time in his life. The challenger failed to go to a neutral corner giving Tunney those vital extra seconds to recover, to get back on his feet after the famous "long count." After ten rounds Tunney remained World's Heavyweight Champion.

The next year Tunney fought Tom Heeney, and after winning by a TKO retired from the ring undefeated.

On October 3, 1928, he married Mary Josephine Lauder, a millionaire's daughter he had fallen in love with and vowed to win. They are the parents of three boys and a girl. In 1964 their oldest boy, John, was elected to the House of Representatives from the State of California.

During World War II Gene served as Director of Athletics and Physical Fitness for the United States Navy. He is the author of two books: *A Man Must Fight* (1932) and *Arms for the Living* (1941).

Gene Tunney made several million dollars in the ring, and after he quit he put it to work for him. He is a director of such companies as the Schick Safety Razor Company, Independent Bank of Commerce, Quaker City Life Insurance, Technicolor, and Eversharp, Inc., as well as others. Gene commutes to his New York office from his Stamford, Connecticut, home daily.

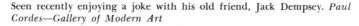

Seen recently enjoying a joke with his old friend, Jack Dempsey. *Paul Cordes—Gallery of Modern Art*

During a 1931 broadcast.

FATHER CHARLES E. COUGHLIN

Father Coughlin made his first radio broadcast in 1926. He confined himself to remarks on morality and Christian virtue. By the early thirties he had become a listening habit to over 30,000,000 Americans on Sunday afternoons, and had turned with passion and eloquence to politics at a time when this country was in the midst of its worst depression.

In 1931, the Columbia Broadcasting System attempted to censor an attack by Coughlin on the Versailles Treaty. Immediately following, the network received 1,250,000 letters of protest against its interference.

At the time of the London Conference on economics in 1933, 85 members of congress petitioned F.D.R. to send the Catholic priest as an official advisor.

In 1934, according to a national poll, Charles E. Coughlin was the second most powerful and popular man in the United States. He was topped only by the President, Coughlin's archfoe, Franklin D. Roosevelt.

In 1935, 20,000 Coughlinites packed Madison Square Garden in New York to hear the priest deliver one of his bitterest attacks on the New Deal. In one of his speeches he referred to President Roosevelt as "the great liar and betrayer." His Bishop, who had up until that time backed him fully, made him apologize to the chief executive. The same year Coughlin referred to Roosevelt as the "Scab President."

In the 1936 elections Coughlin joined forces with Gerald L. K. Smith, and the late Dr. Francis Townsend (father of the Townsend Plan) to form the Union Party. Their candidate, the late Congressman William Lempke, received 900,000 votes. It was during this campaign that Coughlin began to couple his denunciations of President Roosevelt with attacks upon Jewish "bankers." As a result, the Catholic Laymen's League condemned him for "cowardly Jew-baiting and shameless use of the cloth to insult the President."

The National Union for Social Justice with its 8,500,000 members and the *Social Justice* magazine, both under Coughlin's control, continued right up until Pearl Harbor, when the publication was banned by the federal government, and the organization dissolved.

Social Justice was banned from the mails as a result of charges by the Attorney General in April, 1942, as "a systematic and unscrupulous attack upon the war effort." Coughlin condemned the Government's action as the work of "the Jews, Communists and New Dealers."

At the peak of his popularity Father Coughlin's broadcasts, which were heard at 4:00 P.M. E.S.T., were carried over 47 radio stations. Although he was refused a renewal of contract with CBS, independent stations throughout the country formed another network of sorts, and his weekly addresses to the nation continued as usual. His mail reached as high as 1,000,000 letters and cards a week and he retained 4 secretaries and 106 clerks.

Father Coughlin's voice was silenced on the air by his Ecclesiastical superiors in 1940. He continued, however, to speak out on political issues from the pulpit of the Shrine of the Little Flower in Royal Oak, Michigan.

In 1965 parishioners had complained to the Detroit Chancellory office that the Royal Oak pastor had been indoctrinating their children over the public-address system in the parish school. He retired in June of 1966 at the time of his fiftieth anniversary as a priest.

In one of the few interviews the "Radio Priest," as he was called in his heyday, has granted since 1940 he conceded that the transition from a world figure to that of a parish priest had been "a trying one." He allowed that he was for Senator Goldwater in the '64 elections. He had recently been paid a visit from the wife of his old friend, Joseph P. Kennedy.

Father Coughlin lives a short distance from his million-dollar church built by contributions during his days on radio.

In retirement. *Detroit News*

As far back as 1924, Sally was shedding her clothes in *The Dressmaker from Paris*.

SALLY RAND

While still a teenager in the early twenties Sally Rand, who became one of America's most famous strippers, was doing acrobatic dancing at carnivals around the country. She even spent one full season with the Ringling Brothers Circus. It was her agility that got her into pictures playing rough-and-tumble scenes. Throughout the silent era she appeared in many films, the most important of which was the C. B. de Mille classic of 1927 in which she played the handmaiden to the star, Jacqueline Logan, who portrayed Mary Magdalene. The picture was *King of Kings*. Some of Sally's other efforts were *The Dressmaker From Paris* (1924) with Leatrice Joy, *Manbait* (1926) which starred Marie Prevost, *Getting Gertie's Garter* (1927) with Franklin Pangborn in the cast, and *The Fighting Eagle* (1928) with Rod La Rocque.

The girl from Hickory County, Missouri, never achieved stardom in Hollywood. By the time the Depression hit she was stranded in Chicago after a play she was in folded. She took a job dancing in a speakeasy. Trying to save money on costumes she got the idea of using fans. A year later she was doing the same dance in the same club at the same salary—$75.00 a week. When the Chicago World's Fair of 1932–33 was announced Sally tried to land a job at the "Streets of Paris" concession but with no luck.

On the eve of the opening of the Fair, there was a preview for the press and aristocracy of Chicago. Sally invested a week's salary in a white horse and a trailer to transport her to the fairgrounds where, to the amazement of everyone, she did a Lady Godiva act. The next day she was on every front page of every paper in the city. The "Streets of Paris" took her on and the customers poured through the gates to see her, to such an extent that many credit Sally and her fans for the success of the Century of Progress (as the Fair was called) at a time when money was very tight.

After Chicago, Sally toured the United States until 1936, stopping only long enough to appear with George Raft in the 1934 film *Bolero*. Her appearance at the San Diego World's Fair of 1936 set gate records, and in 1939 she repeated the feat at the San Francisco Exposition.

Over the next twenty years she has continued to be a major attraction in burlesque and nightclubs, and still works steadily. When Lyndon Johnson was nominated for the Presidency in 1964 in Atlantic City, Sally Rand was playing the famous Boardwalk. Her act is exactly the same. She still uses Debussy's "Clair de Lune," a Chopin waltz, Ravel, and Brahms for her music. The costume has also remained unchanged—ostrich plumes and not a stitch of clothing. In 1965 when Ann Corio became ill, Sally replaced her as emcee for the successful Broadway revue *This Was Burlesque*.

Not long ago, Sally made a minor stir in Chicago. She was on a television panel program with the columnist Irv Kupicent, and the book *Harlow* was being discussed. Someone mentioned that in the book, which Sally had not yet read, it was stated that Jean Harlow's husband, Paul Bern, had been impotent and that that was probably the reason he had committed suicide. To a rather startled panel and public Miss Rand announced that the author should have checked his facts as they were completely inaccurate. Bern, Sally said, was one of the finest men she had ever known and he was a superb lover as well. No one was more surprised than the author, Irving Shulman, who was a member of the panel that day.

Sally, who admits to being born in 1904, has no intention of putting away her fans. Although her act has grossed several million dollars since she broke out of the South Side Chicago speakeasy and therefore doesn't need the money, she looks forward to her work, the traveling, and to meeting people. In Glendora, California, where she lives with her mother and teenage son, Sally owns a number of pieces of real estate, is a rancher, cultivates citrus orchards, raises chickens, rabbits, and ponies. She has been married several times but is now single. "I lost my last husband," she says jokingly, "lost him to a young girl"—Sally's measurements are 36-24-37.

Still fluttering her fans today.

ALGER HISS

In August of 1948 Whittaker Chambers, a writer and editor and former member of the United States Communist party, told the House Un-American Activities Committee that Alger Hiss had committed treason against the United States of America. Thus began one of the most puzzling and complicated cases in this country's history.

Although Hiss had not been well known to the general public before his name began appearing in the headlines in 1948, he was a prominent figure in and around the federal government, and had been, since he was made law clerk to Justice Oliver Wendell Holmes in 1929 at the suggestion of Felix Frankfurter. He had been also one of the "bright young men" around F.D.R., and was present at the Dumbarton Oaks talks and at Roosevelt's meeting with Churchill and Stalin at Yalta.

Hiss was born in Baltimore in 1904 and attended Harvard Law School. He had acted as counsel to the Nye Committee during its investigations of the munitions industry in 1934 and 1935. In 1936 he was made an assistant to Francis B. Sayre, Assistant Secretary of State. He specialized in Far Eastern Affairs, and eventually became Director of that office in the State Department. At the first meeting of the United Nations in San Francisco he was named as temporary Secretary General.

There were accusations, denials, counteraccusations, and endless hearings. Chambers and Hiss stood face to face, and repeated what is undoubtedly the most conflicting testimony any congressional committee, and perhaps any court, has ever heard. Chambers said that Hiss had been his closest friend while they were Communists. Hiss said that he was not and never had been a Communist and that he did not know Whittaker Chambers. The only thing that was certain was that one of them was the coolest, most calculating liar on record. Further to confuse the press and public, both men seemed on the surface and by their records to be quite well balanced and intelligent, and during their testimony appeared straightforward and sincere.

It was high drama but no play or movie ever had such a bizarre plot. A few of the props which were to become world famous were the Woodstock typewriter #230,099, a 1929 Ford which Hiss thrice denied owning, and the most incredible of all—the "pumpkin papers," State Department documents on microfilm that Chambers turned up on his farm hidden in a hollowed-out pumpkin. Among the cast of characters was a young California Congressman full of questions for the witnesses and statements for the press, Richard M. Nixon.

Hiss was indicted on a count of perjury. His first trial in June, 1949, ended in a hung jury. A second jury convicted him in November, 1949, and he served 44 months at the federal prison in Lewisburg, Pennsylvania.

16

While in prison, in 1952, Hiss was denied a motion for a new trial. After his release, August 25, 1954, he worked as office manager for a small New York firm. He and his wife separated, and are still living apart. His son Tony attended Harvard on a scholarship and is now on the staff of a top national magazine.

In May, 1957, Hiss's book *In the Court of Public Opinion* was published, one of the most eagerly awaited books in years. It was disappointing in every way, including sales, being little more than a legal brief of the trials. Even his strongest supporters had to admit that it offered no new evidence. Hiss's answer to the criticism was that it was not written for money.

The entire affair has been compared with the Dreyfus case in France, but Hiss has refused to be treated as a *cause célèbre*. One writer referred to him as: "rather than a martyr—the man is the non-hero of his own case."

When Hiss discusses the case it is with a peculiar detachment. He has stated that since he knows he is innocent of the charges he is convinced that he will eventually be cleared. When asked about the evidence presented by the prosecution he refers you to his book. When queried about new evidence of his innocence he says it must wait to be presented at the new trial his lawyers still hope to get. (Chambers died several years ago.)

He stopped granting interviews after his book came out and explains in a gentlemanly fashion that he is now a private citizen and as such will not permit his privacy to be invaded. The last time he appeared on radio or television was shortly after Richard Nixon was defeated in his race for the California governorship in 1962. His comments on the former Vice-President's career and character, solicited by a newsman, drew objections from many groups and individuals including Dwight D. Eisenhower.

Alger Hiss since 1960 has been an office supply salesman for a stationery company in New York City. He looks very much like the same tall gaunt figure that dominated the news so much in the late forties. There is no trace of bitterness, and the slightly arrogant manner he displayed on the witness stand is gone. He is, in fact, charming and unusually polite.

In 1948, at the time Whittaker Chambers made his accusations, Hiss was serving as President of the Carnegie Endowment for International Peace. *Culver Pictures*

A theatre and symphony patron (*right*), frequently recognized. *UPI*

Probably the most popular man in pre-Hitler Germany, World Heavyweight Champion, 1930. *Ring Magazine*

MAX SCHMELING

The only German to become the World's Heavyweight Champion was born in Brandenburg in 1905. He began boxing in 1924 and developed a reputation for having a deadly punch and an amazing ability to withstand punishment. Before coming to America in 1928, he was also known for two disqualifications for fouling, a lost decision to Jack Taylor, and losing to the Englishman Gypsy Daniels.

The first thing sportswriters noticed about Max was his facial resemblance to Jack Dempsey, but they soon discovered that he had more than looks to qualify him for main events. In 1929 he KO'd Joe Monte in the eighth round and flattened Johnny Risko, something even Gene Tunney was unable to do, although he beat Risko.

When Tunney retired in 1928 the title was up for grabs, and there were few around of championship stock. One was Spaniard Paulino Uzcudun until Schmeling beat him, thereby becoming one of the top contenders. He was sidetracked for the time being, however, when England's Heavyweight Champion Phil Scott got first crack at leading contender, Jack Sharkey, in 1930. (Although Sharkey won the match he made a poor showing).

When Sharkey and Schmeling finally entered the ring on July 12, 1930, in New York City the odds were on the German. The winner of the match was to receive the title that had gone begging since Tunney had called it quits. The gate was $749,935, a hefty gross even in good times, and this was one of the worst years of the Depression. For the first three rounds Sharkey was ahead on points, although Max was aggressive and obviously in good form. Then in the fourth round Sharkey let go with a wild wandering punch that landed on Schmeling's stomach and sent him to the canvas. Though probably unintentional, the blow was a foul one, and by virtue of its illegality Max Schmeling was crowned the new Champion.

18

After a visit home to Germany—where Adolf Hitler cited him as a perfect example of the Aryan superman—Max was matched in July, 1931, against Young Stribling in Cleveland, who lasted until the middle of the 15th round when the fight was stopped by the referee and declared a victory for Schmeling on a TKO. Most of the experts had picked the challenger.

In June, 1932, a startled crowd in New York City heard Jack Sharkey proclaimed the new Champion after 15 rounds, during which, according to just about everyone's scorecard, Max had outpointed him. It was a bitterly disputed decision and a sour chapter in the annals of boxing.

In September, 1932, Schmeling knocked out former Middleweight Champion Mickey Walker. In June the following year Max Baer did as much for Schmeling by stopping him in the tenth round.

When Schmeling met Joe Louis in June, 1936, the press referred to Max as "the condemned man." So heavy were the odds on the young Negro that it cut the gate a quarter of a million dollars below expectations. Some 42,000 spectators sat dumbfounded as the German KO'd the Brown Bomber in one of the sport's biggest upsets. Contrary to what everyone had expected—it seemed perfectly reasonable—Max was not given a chance at the title, which, since 1935, was held by Braddock. Also, anti-German feelings were running high in the United States, and at his advanced age Braddock seemed a setup for just about anyone.

In 1938, a year after he had taken the title from Jim Braddock, Joe Louis and Schmeling were rematched. Max's attempt to regain the title resulted in a humiliating defeat for him when the Champion knocked him out in two minutes and four seconds in the first round.

Schmeling returned to Germany where he continued to box until he was drafted into the army. He was reported killed in 1941 while a member of Hitler's paratroopers invading Crete. It turned out that it was only a leg injury and not even a bad enough one to keep him from teaching boxing in his homeland for a while after the war ended. A few years ago his fortunes took a turn for the better when he was named an executive of the Coca-Cola bottling works at Essen, Germany, a position he still holds.

Former heavyweight champion of Germany, Albert Westphal, listens to some advice from an elder statesman of boxing. *Wide World*

Miss America of 1919 is presented with a golden apple, the symbol of her title. She is surrounded by prominent artists of the day: (*left to right*) Harrison Fischer, Penshyn Stanlaws, James Montgomery Flagg, and, kneeling, Howard Chandler Christy.

MISS AMERICA OF 1919

Though an unofficial event (nor was there a contest in 1920), the first Miss America was chosen by a group of the most distinguished artists in the country at the Chu Chin Chow Ball, held in the Hotel des Artistes on Central Park West in New York. The date was February 1, 1919. All the contestants (who included movie and Ziegfeld beauties Hazel Dawn, recently retired from a New York ad agency, Mary Eaton, and Mary Hay) wore costumes.

It was all so casual in those days that the title went to a girl who couldn't really have been "Miss" anything. She was at the time a married woman and a mother of two. Her husband was Tod Robbins, a Riviera playboy, and author of *Freaks* and *The Unholy Three*. Miss America's photograph, taken a month after she won the award, was the first ever to be transmitted from New York to Chicago by a revolutionary process called "wirephoto" which had then just been perfected. It appeared in newspapers and magazines more because of her beauty than title, since the country was not yet used to the pageant as an annual event.

Shortly after being chosen, Edith Hyde (the name she gave reporters at the time—actually it was her maiden name) divorced her writer-husband.

Offers poured in from vaudeville, movies, and the stage. One, who was quite persistent in his attempts to get the young lady in one of his shows, was Florenz Ziegfeld, at a time when he was at the height of his fame and power. In those days, however, going on the stage for a well-bred girl was frowned upon. Edith told the producers that because of her family name and her children she couldn't possibly consider a theatrical career.

20

The real reason, and one she will admit readily to today, is that she had developed a taste for the very thing that had just become illegal in the U.S. —liquor. Very little else mattered.

Along with great beauty, Edith had been gifted with clairvoyance. She began at first just for fun to give friends readings with a deck of cards. The cards were used more as a prop than a guide. Edith had an uncanny ability to predict the future and advise merely by sensing the person's "aura." Her accuracy became quite well known among café society. Her services were in such demand that just to discourage so many people from asking for readings she set a fee. Those who had been embarrassed to ask her when she charged nothing now called at once.

During the twenties Edith worked at her readings in various night clubs around Manhattan. She developed a huge clientele of free-spending celebrities and wealthy people who came back over and over again. The table that she occupied was never far from the bar.

It has now been twenty years since Edith Hyde Robbins Macartney has had a drink. She was by her own admission "a complete alcoholic for years." With the help of friends she regained her sobriety, and she claims to have been able to stay sober by helping others who have had a problem with alcohol.

The first Miss America lives near Sutton Place in Manhattan only a block away from her first son, who is a songwriter. Her second boy is an executive with an advertising agency.

When Edith stopped drinking she left night clubs. She now works at the Gypsy Tea Room on Broadway in New York. She is there every day working under the name of "Pandora." Many of her old clients, some of Broadway and Hollywood's biggest names, still consult her regularly.

"Pandora" today.

CHARLES A. LINDBERGH

The greatest hero of them all was born in Detroit, Michigan, in 1902. He was brought up in Nebraska, where he became an Air Mail pilot, stunt flier, and barnstormer during days when aviation was still at a primitive stage.

On May 20, 1927, Lindbergh took off in a plane he named "The Spirit of St. Louis," bound for Paris. No one had made it before, and few gave this young man much of a chance to make the 3,600-mile journey nonstop. Then news came across the wires that he had landed at Le Bourget Airport after 33½ hours in the air. From that moment on it was like all the celebrations ever known or heard of happening at once. Not just in Paris or the United States but all over the world in every town and city bells rang, whistles sounded, and people were near hysteria. What they said couldn't be done and shouldn't be attempted had been done by a slim young American.

Charles Lindbergh seemed everything one could ask for in a hero. He was tall, blond, and handsome. He came from a good middle-class home, and perhaps what made him loved and cheered more than anything else was that he seemed embarrassed and a little frightened by it all.

After the crowned heads of Europe had a brief glimpse of him, a cruiser sent by President Coolidge brought him back home to a welcome never before nor since accorded anyone. There were receptions and parades in 100 cities. He refused offers totaling over 7½ million dollars and gave to a museum gifts he received worth over 2 million dollars.

In 1929 he married Anne Morrow, the daughter of the United States Ambassador to Mexico, and three years later the most admired man in the world was subjected to the vilest crime on earth. His son, Charles, Jr., was kidnapped and later found dead. In a sensational trial, Bruno Richard Hauptmann was convicted of the crime and subsequently electrocuted, but the Lindberghs were still plagued with threats against the lives of their other children. In 1935 he took his family to live in England.

During a trip to Germany in 1938, Lindbergh was decorated with the Service Cross of the German Eagle by the No. 2 Nazi, Hermann Göring. It has been alleged that Lindbergh had not been warned that this was going to happen and did not understand the speech Field Marshal Göring made preceding the presentation Lindbergh was severely criticized for accepting. Nonetheless, upon his return to the United States in the late thirties, the celebrated flier began to make isolationist speeches for the America First Committee. When President Roosevelt criticized him on April 25, 1941, for his isolationist stance, Lindbergh resigned his commission.

Several months later, in a speech he made at a nationally broadcast America First Committee rally in Des Moines, Iowa, Lindbergh charged that, "The three most important groups who have been pressing this country toward war are the British, the Jews and the Roosevelt administration. . . ." He stated that ". . . their [the Jews'] greatest danger to this country lies in their large ownership and influence in our motion pictures, our press, our radio and our government. . . ."

Lindbergh was condemned for attempting to inject anti-Semitism into the issues of the day. The New York *Herald Tribune* said that in doing so Lindbergh had "sinned against the American spirit." The New York *Journal American* (a Hearst paper) said that "the raising of a racial issue by Lindbergh was the most unfortunate happening in the United States since the present tense international situation developed."

Although never officially a member of any of the Armed Forces during the Second World War, Lindbergh flew many dangerous missions in the South Pacific and received the Congressional Medal of Honor after V-J. Day.

Both the kidnapping and the treatment by the press and public for his antiwar sentiments left the Lone Eagle a man determined to avoid publicity. He grants no interviews of any kind and makes very few public appearances. When Lindbergh finally got around to writing his story *The Spirit of St. Louis* in 1954 it won the Pulitzer Prize and was a best seller; the movie made from it in 1957 starring Jimmy Stewart was a financial failure.

Lindbergh lives in Darien, Connecticut, with his wife, three sons, and two daughters. Although it is never publicized, he is a consultant and a director of Pan-American Airways, and makes trips around the world for them as often as several times a month. He keeps a small house in Switzerland which he and his wife use for their writing. Lindbergh is an enthusiastic skin diver and skier, and he has never smoked nor tasted alcohol in his life. He has long ago reaccepted his old commission in the Air Force and is now a Brigadier General. He was among the group who selected the site for the Air Force Academy, and was a member of the committee that advised the go-ahead of the Atlas missile project.

His mail in 1927 ran to nearly 4 million pieces. It contained over $100,000 just in return postage. He now receives nearly 1,000 cards and letters a week, none of which he opens. Like all his papers, and much of his memorabilia, they go into a large vault at Yale University.

Perhaps the first man on the moon will be acclaimed as Charles Augustus Lindbergh was—it is to be hoped that fate will be kinder to him than it was to "Lucky Lindy."

In 1927 beside his famous monoplane, now hanging from the ceiling of the Smithsonian Institution in Washington, D.C., and *(right)* today a director of Pan-American.

Underwood & Underwood   *UPI*

The Presidental candidate in 1936.

ALFRED M. LANDON

During the campaign of 1936 President Roosevelt made a remark about Landon's symbol, the sunflower. He said it was only good for parrot food. That is about as personal as the race ever got. One New Deal historian wrote that when Landon and F.D.R. met in the middle of the campaign they got on so well one observer said he was surprised one of them didn't withdraw from the race.

Although he was a comparative unknown when the powerful Senator Borah threw his support to the Kansas Governor, he came up as the winner on the first ballot at the G.O.P. Convention. His running mate was the late Frank Knox, who was later to serve in F.D.R.'s cabinet. Landon fought a vigorous campaign, and criticized every point of the New Deal program with the exception of its farm relief.

It is assumed that Alf Landon felt he could win, but—whether because of the Democrats or in spite of them—the economy was beginning to rally and the voters did not want to chance a change in direction.

Not even Barry Goldwater's defeat in 1964 was as decisive as the Roosevelt landslide that buried Landon. He lost every state but Maine and Vermont with a popular vote of 27,751,597 to 16,679,583. In the electoral college the incumbent candidate received 523 with 8 going to the G.O.P. One of the most personally satisfying aspects of the tally to President Roosevelt was that it was the first and only time he ever carried his home district in New York.

In spite of the lopsided results of the elections, as late as October bets were being made in New York with Landon getting even odds. The newspapers were for the most part supporting him and *The Literary Digest,* a leading magazine of the day, announced the results of its poll—he would most certainly be our next President.

At the time it seemed that Landon had a good chance to unseat F.D.R. James A. Farley, Roosevelt's campaign manager and one of the smartest political observers of any year, did not take Alfred Mossman Landon lightly.

Not only would the Democratic ticket have the Union party (Coughlin, Smith, and Townsend) to contend with, but Al Smith's Jeffersonian Democrats were sitting this one out after Smith "took a walk" at the Democratic Convention.

The final figures showed that many crossed party lines in 1936. The one conversion of note that Alf Landon accomplished was to be an important one four years later when Wendell L. Willkie admitted that although he had been a registered Democrat until then, he had voted for the Republican ticket that year. Although Landon left public office in 1937, at the 1940 convention he was Kansas' favorite son candidate, and after holding out for several roll calls gave Willkie his support, becoming one of the candidate's most effective stumpers in the Midwest during the campaign.

Since 1937 Alf Landon has become a prominent figure in Kansas business. He is at last President—president of the radio stations he owns in Dodge City, Liberal, and Topeka, Kansas. He lives in Topeka where part of his time is taken up by the several oil, gas, and real-estate properties he owns.

Much to the surprise of the audience at a S.A.N.E. rally, he appeared on the speakers' platform alongside Mrs. Eleanor Roosevelt and he supported Lyndon B. Johnson in the 1964 elections.

A prominent businessman today.
Topeka Capital Journal

In the early 1940's.

ROCKWELL KENT

Rockwell Kent, born in Tarrytown, New York, in 1882, has become one of the best known, most versatile, and most controversial artists this country has ever produced.

Over his long career he has worked in watercolor, pen and ink, lithography, wood block, and oil—all with equal skill. Kent combines the classic in form with the romantic in feeling, and is represented in various media in the permanent collections of both the Metropolitan Museum of Art, and the Whitney Museum in New York City, the Gallery of Fine Arts in Columbus, Ohio, the Brooklyn Museum, New York, the Art Institute of Chicago, the Pushkin Museum of Moscow, and the Hermitage in Leningrad. He is one of the highest paid illustrators in commercial art, some of his work being the design of corporative advertisements seen in magazines.

Kent studied at Columbia University, and was the pupil of Kenneth Hayes Miller, Abbott H. Thayer, Robert Henri, and William Chase, prominent names in American art at the beginning of the twentieth century. Although he made his debut as an artist in 1910, he did not become well known until his first book *Wilderness, a Journal of Quiet Adventure in Alaska* was published in 1920. He followed this success with another travel book in 1924, *Voyaging*, which was set in Tierra del Fuego. His later books on wanderings were *N by E* (1930) about Greenland, and *Salamina* (1935), named for his Eskimo housekeeper in Alaska. He also wrote *Rockwellkentiana* (1933), a book about his pictures with reprints of criticisms of them.

Although artistically conservative, Rockwell Kent has been known as the "stormy petrel of the art world" for his liberal politics. He has written irate letters over the years to just about every conservative journal in the country; at the time of the execution of Sacco and Vanzetti in 1927, he sent a blistering letter of resignation to the Worcester Museum in Massachusetts, and he was passionately devoted to the cause of the Loyalist government in Spain during the Civil War.

In 1938 he incorporated an inflammatory message in an obscure Eskimo

26

dialect into a mural on the wall of the United States post office in Washington, D.C. The painting pictured a United States mailman delivering mail to Puerto Ricans. A letter read: "To the People of Puerto Rico, our friends! Go ahead. Let us change chiefs. That alone can make us free." After a loud uproar from political quarters it was finally removed.

He has lectured extensively and is the author of two very well received autobiographies, *This Is My Own* (1940) and *It's Me, O Lord* (1955).

Kent has been the subject for congressional investigations on several occasions. Joseph McCarthy, the Wisconsin senator, was one of those who accused the artist of fellow-traveling. In 1953 Kent's name figured in the congressional inquiry over alleged Communist writers in the State Department libraries overseas. Although he has stated publicly that he does not believe in a form of Russian communism for the United States, he took the Fifth Amendment when asked under oath whether or not he was or ever had been a member of the Communist party. He still denies party membership.

Before Americans were permitted by their government to travel behind the Iron Curtain, Kent defied the ban and attended a number of Communist-sponsored rallies in Eastern Europe. When he returned to the United States the State Department voided his passport. In 1958, after nearly eight years of litigation in federal courts, the Supreme Court granted Kent another passport, stating that he was entitled to the document in spite of his associations. He testified at the time that he was "only working for peace" and knew "very little about the Communist party." Upon hearing the decision Kent said, "I am one American who does not like having his corns stepped on . . . be yourself, be yourself as an artist, be yourself as a man."

His illustrations for Voltaire's *Candide* (1928), Wilder's *Bridge of San Luis Rey* (1929), Chaucer's *Canterbury Tales* (1930), Shakespearean plays, Melville's *Moby Dick* (1931) and an edition of *Beowulf* have kept these editions in print throughout the years.

Kent has remained very busy with art commissions for nearly a half century, and though he has been less productive and less vocal in recent years, he still does occasional illustrations, and holds very strong opinions on current events. He lives quietly in Ausable Forks, New York.

At home recently in Ausable Forks.

In 1925, United States Amateur Champ.

BOBBY JONES

Golf's immortal, Robert Tyre Jones, Jr., was born on St. Patrick's Day in Atlanta, Georgia, in 1902. At the age of seven he was practicing his swing; at twelve he posted a notice on the bulletin board in his father's club, "Out in 36, back in 24," thereby tying the amateur record for the course.

Though even while in school Bobby was copping titles such as the Southern Amateur Golf Championship of 1917, 1920, and 1922, throughout his teenage years he lost tournament after tournament and was becoming better known for his fits of temper than for his mettle. In 1922, however, he tied for second place with Gene Sarazen in the Open at Skokie, and from then on his tantrums subsided and his fame spread. That same year he was graduated as a mechanical engineer from the Georgia Institute of Technology, and two years later received a B.S. from Harvard.

There were an estimated 250,000 golfers in this country in 1915. By 1925 there were five million. The rise can be attributed to the prosperity of the twenties and the additional leisure time—and to the admiration the public had developed for Bobby Jones. Paul Gallico said of him, "He was the finest golfer and competitor ever produced in the United States or anywhere else, the King himself of the Golden People."

A typical example of his sense of fair play is when in the 1925 United States Open Championship, Bobby called a penalty stroke on himself which seemed so severe that he was called before the officials and asked if he had actually taken his stance. After some discussion and much amazement on the part of the crowd—and cynical sportswriters—the penalty was allowed to stand. It inspired one newspaperman to call him "the best sportsman, the greatest gentleman, and the champion of champions." Ten years after retirement Jones was still being lauded by those who knew him during his days of competition. In 1940 Grantland Rice wrote: "There is no more chance that golf will give the world another Jones than there is that literature will produce another Shakespeare."

From 1923 through 1929 Jones took slightly more than a trophy a year: He won the United States Open Championship in 1923, 1926, and 1929; the United States Amateur Championship in 1924, 1925, 1927, and 1928; the British Open in 1926 and 1927.

In 1930, after confiding only to his father what his goal was that year ("I felt myself reluctant to admit that I considered myself capable of such an accomplishment"), he won the grand slam of golf by taking the British Open, with a score of 291; the British Amateur; the United States Open Championship at Interlachen, with a 287; and the United States Amateur Championship at Merion Country Club in Ardmore, Pennsylvania.

When he came back to this country—halfway on his way to the grand slam—he was met by Grover Whelan, who took him from his liner onto a tug that brought him to the Battery to be greeted by Mayor Jimmy Walker. Jones was seated in the Mayor's car, and the two proceeded to drive northward on the isle of Manhattan for a ticker tape parade that still ranks as one of the city's biggest and most enthusiastic.

Jones retired from competition after his 1930 triumph but was a familiar face on the links until 1948, when he was first stricken with a spinal ailment which has grown increasingly worse over the years until he is now confined to a wheel chair.

Bobby is the father of two girls and a boy, is a member of the Georgia Bar Association, until recently practicing out of his father's Atlanta office, is a Vice President of the A. G. Spaulding Company and a board member and founder of the Augusta National Golf Club, one of Dwight Eisenhower's favorite haunts.

He has written several books including *Golf Is My Game,* and has just contributed a foreword to a large illustrated book on the history of the game.

A corporation vice-president today. *U.S. Golf Association*

ALEXANDER KERENSKY

Had events gone just a bit more favorably for him, Alexander Kerensky might today be a major Russian political figure, and the world divided much differently from the way it now is. Kerensky was born in Simbirsk, Russia, in 1881, the son of a minor nobleman. After studying law he gained a reputation for his frequent and skillful defense of socialists who were constantly being arrested by the police of Russia's last Czar, Nicolas II.

After the Socialist Revolution party was outlawed he was elected in 1912 as a Labor party member of the fourth State Duma. Although rather young at the time, he achieved respect and fame as an orator and mediator.

After the Revolution of 1917 Kerensky was named to the post of Minister of Justice in the first Provisional Government, and was simultaneously one of the Vice-Presidents of the Petrograd (Leningrad) Soviet. After the resignation of the Liberal party ministers he became Minister of War on May 5, 1917, and prepared the renewal of offensive action on the front against Germany and Austria-Hungary. In his speeches and pronouncements he attempted to rally the Russian people to continue a war of which they had long before wearied.

On July 17, 1917, he ordered Cossack troops to Petrograd in order to smash the first attempt of the Bolsheviks to seize power. At the same time he was responsible for freeing some of the top Bolshevik leaders, one of whom was Leon Trotsky, who had been arrested after another unsuccessful uprising.

After the reorganization of the Provisional Government Kerensky became Prime Minister of Russia on July 25, 1917. The following September he and General Kornilov, supreme commander of the Russian armed forces, clashed when the General wanted to make the government into something close to a dictatorship. During this quarrel Kerensky ordered the arming of the factory workers of Petrograd, who in a few months' time were to turn against him and his government. After futile attempts to maintain his government in power he proclaimed Russia a republic. The order was challenged as unconstitutional.

On November 6, 1917, the second Bolshevik revolt broke out. Kerensky fled the capital, ostensibly to bring loyal troops to the defense of Petrograd. The move failed, and he left Russia for the last time.

In early 1918 Kerensky turned up in London, and joined the campaign against the new Soviet government, but his policies and acts during his tenure of office made no friends for him among the White Russians who were the strongest group advocating the liberation of their homeland.

Until the Germans invaded France in 1940 Kerensky lived and worked in Paris. He was the editor of a Socialist Revolutionary newspaper *Dni*. Some of the books he wrote during that period were *Prelude to Bolshevism* in 1919 and *Catastrophe* in 1927.

Kerensky has been living in the United States since 1940. Although he has always been a bitter critic of Stalin and his policies, when the Nazis invaded Russia in 1940 he pleaded with the United States Government for aid and with the American people for private contributions for Russian Relief.

In 1965 an account of his life as head of the Russian government was published in the United States. While he granted some interviews to publicize the book, *Russia and History's Turning Point,* it was with the understanding that all questions were to be submitted to him beforehand. Most critics complained that the book historians had long awaited contained no answers to the key questions that had gone unanswered for so long.

Kerensky is still defensive about the accusations made over the years by White Russians as well as objective observers that his government, because of its vacillation and indecision, was directly responsible for the success of Lenin.

Since he has been in this country Kerensky has contributed an occasional article to national magazines on the changes in Russian foreign and domestic policies, and lectured at various universities. Until recently he was with the Library for the Study of War and Revolution in Palo Alto, California, a foundation set up by Herbert C. Hoover, former United States President. Kerensky is currently conducting classes on Russian history at Stanford University in California.

At his office at the Socialist Revolutionary newspaper, Paris, 1918.
John P. Gilligan

At his home recently, Berkeley, California.

MARTIN DIES

Martin Dies was born in Colorado, Texas, in 1901. His father, Martin Dies, Sr., who served in Congress for ten years, had been an outspoken opponent of America's entry into World War I.

By the time Congressman Dies was nineteen years old he was practicing law in Texas; at thirty the Democrat was elected to the House of Representatives. At the time he was considered to be a protégé of Texan John Nance Garner. Throughout President Roosevelt's first term in office Dies supported most of the New Deal legislation. By 1936, however, it was clear that Martin Dies was a political maverick.

Once Dies began to differ with the party leadership his flair for making headlines became obvious. One of his well-publicized ideas concerned the high unemployment rate at the height of the Depression. The Texas Congressman suggested that the federal government make more jobs available to native-born Americans by deporting the six million aliens living in the United States at the time. In 1936 Dies lashed out against the unions during the bitter General Motors sit-down strikes. In 1937 he followed the lead of Vice-President Garner in his opposition to F.D.R.'s plan to pack the Supreme Court.

Communist and Fascist groups in the United States had been investigated with fanfare by other politicians but Dies went about it with an expertise and sense of publicity that was not to be equaled until the advent of Joseph McCarthy. In May, 1938, the House Un-American Activities Committee was created by Congress with an appropriation of $25,000 with Dies as chairman. So strongly did he dominate its workings and its headlines that it was referred to as the Dies Committee. From its very inception the Committee was criticized by liberals, leftists, and members of Congress from both parties. In spite of the attacks on its tactics and the dearth of genuine subversion it exposed, the Committee had its budget increased to $100,000 by 1939.

A few of the things that came under its scrutiny were the W.P.A. Federal Theatre and Writers' Project, the National Labor Relations Board, the Department of Labor, the Workers' Alliance, and the American Youth Congress.

One of the criticisms leveled at the Committee was that it seemed obsessed with communism while paying too little attention to the organizations that were admittedly Fascist and Nazi in the United States prior to Pearl Harbor. Dies ignored the denouncements of civil libertarians and unions such as the C.I.O. who claimed that his investigations infringed on the rights of Amercans. One of his statements is characteristic of his intentions and philosophy: "America is a free country and I would defend with my life the rights of its citizens, but when they take the oath of allegiance and seek to undermine our government I say what amendment in our Constitution protects these spies and agents of foreign governments?"

In 1940 he wrote a book called *Trojan Horse in America* which outlined the plan, according to Dies, of foreign powers to infiltrate and take over the United States Government. When it was pointed out to him that the country already had a number of investigative branches that were perhaps much better equipped to protect us than his Committee, Dies stated that the F.B.I. was ineffectual in comparison to the results achieved by his Committee.

In 1945 he decided against running for reelection, and returned to Texas and the practice of law. In 1953 he was reelected to Congress and served until 1959, thereafter retiring from politics and returning to Texas.

Since leaving the House, Dies has been writing for a number of right wing journals, and in 1963 wrote another version of his Committee's work entitled *The Martin Dies Story*. Dies continues to practice law in Lufkin, Texas, and spends some time hunting and shooting pool. When asked for a comment on the current political scene the former Congressman replied, "I think we have scraped the bottom of the barrel."

In 1938 at the height of his fame and power, and (*right*) today in Lufkin, Texas.

Mowan Studio

In 1935 she played the title role in the film *She*. RKO

HELEN GAHAGAN DOUGLAS

Few personalities have had as varied a public life as this lady, becoming a success in politics long before entertainers were being taken seriously by the voting public. She began life as the daughter of a wealthy conservative Republican family and became a staunch New Dealer. On Broadway and in Europe she starred both as a singer and an actress. Some of her legitimate stage work was *Manhattan* (1922), her first, *Trelawney of the Wells* (1926), *Tonight or Never* (1930), and *The Cat and the Fiddle* (1932).

Although she appeared in only one film, the 1935 production of *She*, it became a science-fiction classic and had to be withdrawn from release so that it would not compete with a recent remake.

When she moved to Los Angeles in the thirties Helen became interested in social work. In 1939 she was involved with the New Deal as part of an advisory group for the Works Progress Administration and the National Youth Administration.

Her political career as an elected official started in 1945 when she began serving as Congresswoman from a working-class district in Los Angeles. She was the "Democrats' answer to Clare Boothe Luce" in the House of Representatives in the 79th to 81st Congresses. Much to the distress of the press there was no battle of the beauties while they served in the House together. Even when Mrs. Douglas was named to the Best Dressed Women list, an honor Mrs. Luce had enjoyed many times, no cattiness developed. Recently Mrs. Douglas remarked, "I didn't feel at all competitive. She was always better dressed than I was." The two ladies had a mutual respect for each other which has lasted through the years.

34

In 1950 Mrs. Douglas ran for the Senate of the United States from California on the Democratic ticket against a young Congressman fresh from triumph in the Alger Hiss inquiry. The contest is still remembered as one of the dirtiest ever waged in that state because of her opponent's insinuations and tactics. The winner by a wide margin was the future Vice-President Richard M. Nixon.

About her feelings concerning Mr. Nixon now that so many years have passed, she said: "I really feel sorry for him. The election was at the time of the Korean War. The Democrats were on the defensive. I really think he probably would have won anyway."

Helen Gahagan Douglas lives in a large apartment overlooking the Hudson River in New York City with her husband, Melvyn Douglas, whom she married in 1932. They are proud grandparents. She is still popular as a lecturer on humanitarian causes and a fund raiser for the Democratic party. Although she doesn't rule out a return to the theatre she seems much more interested in assisting local candidates. Her last Broadway appearances were *First Lady* (1952) and *Family Reunion* (1954).

For all the time that has passed since she entered public life Helen feels that her ideas have changed very little: "I'm afraid that you can still put me down as a liberal. I can see, however, that there is often more than one answer to a problem—not always but often. And I am constantly surprised to find how really conservative the so-called liberals are that I meet. And the conservatives, I'm pleased to find, they are often not nearly so Right as I've been led to believe."

Mrs. Douglas is
now a grandmother.

Her comeback film in 1932, *A Woman Commands*, is memorable only for the song she introduced in it, "Paradise." *RKO*

POLA NEGRI

The famous silent picture star was born Appolonia Chalupec in Poland. She was well established in Europe through her films *Gypsy Blood* and *Passion* when she came to Hollywood in 1921 with her director, the talented Ernst Lubitsch.

Paramount Pictures, the studio that brought her to this country and spent a fortune to promote her, gave her such vehicles as *The Last Payment* (1922), *The Red Peacock* (1922), and *Hotel Imperial* (1927). Pola was the first to complain that her American-made pictures were inferior. Quick to second her were the critics and public.

Although Paramount was never quite able to put her across, she made many pictures for them. By the late twenties the star who was once thought to be a threat to Gloria Swanson was so unpopular with the exhibitors that some refused to feature her name in their advertising.

Pola Negri's life in her films and in her personal world were hard to distinguish. It was a toss-up which was the more dramatic. On the screen she was the Vamp who led her prey into danger and sin. And yet she too suffered for her deeds. In *Men* (1924) the advertising copy read: "the woman who pays and makes men pay." When Valentino died suddenly in New York in 1926 she left a movie in the middle of production, rushed across the country, and threw herself on his casket. When Gloria Swanson married a Marquis, Pola countered by wedding a prince. She had been married to a Polish count before that.

In spite of a disappointing career in this country Pola Negri is one of the handful of silent stars whose names are known to young people today. It is a great tribute to her as a personality because, unlike many silent stars, her films are seldom shown at art houses or film festivals. She had great beauty, enormous glamour, and a sense of publicity second to none.

After her dismal failure in Hollywood talkies she went back to Europe where she worked mostly in Germany during the thirties in films and cabarets. The recordings that she made during that period in her deep Slavic accent are still for sale in Germany rerecorded from the old 78's onto LP's.

Even in the twilight of her career before the Second World War Pola Negri was able to manage a headline now and then. Somehow the press learned that no less a personage than Adolf Hitler was enamored with her. When questioned she replied, "Why not? All of the men in my life have been important men. Take Valentino, for instance."

Pola returned to this country just before the fall of France in 1940, penniless, her career over. Thanks to the generosity of a close friend, with whom she lived quietly since retiring and who has recently died, she is financially secure with a beautiful home in San Antonio, Texas, and a trust fund.

Today Pola spends most of her time writing her autobiography.
Walt Disney Productions

JOHN L. LEWIS

The labor leader whose power was for a time second only to that of the President of the United States was born in Iowa in 1880. His parents had come to this country from Wales, and his father was for a time on a blacklist put out by the mine operators after he had protested working conditions in the pits.

John Llewellyn attended school for only seven years before he, too, became a coal miner. In 1906 he was named a delegate of the United Mine Workers, and traveled around the country talking with the miners, and observing the deplorable conditions that existed.

In 1918 he became Vice-President, and two years later was President. From the very beginning it was obvious to the mine operators that they were not dealing with any ordinary labor agitator. During negotiations they were amazed by his huge vocabulary and dramatic manner. John L. also set to work consolidating his power within the union.

It was during the New Deal that Lewis' power and fury really were felt in the nation. He supported F.D.R.'s first two terms with funds from the union's treasury, and his own oratorical skills. The Vice-President, a conservative, was another matter. He called John Nance Garner, "a labor-baiting, poker-playing, whiskey-drinking, evil old man."

In 1935 he split with the A. F. of L. and formed the C.I.O. Lewis had wanted to organize unskilled labor, and the A. F. of L. was interested only in trade unionists. Under Lewis' leadership the C.I.O. organized with enormous success, notably in Detroit, where the sit-down strikes brought scab workers that in turn brought violence, ending in state troopers being called in.

In 1938 Lewis and F.D.R. broke while Lewis was scrapping with the steel industry. He had expected the President's help and instead received the famous curse, "a plague on both your houses."

Seldom have two adversaries been more perfectly matched than Lewis and Roosevelt, both colorful, both powerful, and each a master at insult and mockery. In attempting to keep F.D.R. from becoming President again Lewis made his biggest mistake. When it became obvious that Roosevelt was going to run for a third term Lewis backed the G.O.P. candidate Wendell L. Willkie, and promised to resign if the Republican candidate was not elected. He quit as President of the C.I.O. in 1940 and to this day his union has remained aloof from the subsequent A.F.L.-C.I.O. merger.

He pulled his miners out of the pits during the Second World War, probably making him the most unpopular man in the nation. Several times the government took over the mines, and once a federal judge assessed him and his union a combined $2,130,000 in fines for ignoring a court order to return to work.

While many former miners accuse John L. of a "sellout" during the last years of his reign, most observers feel that his agreement to allow automation in the mines was the only sensible thing he could do. Oil, gas, and atomic power had begun to replace "King Coal" in many industries, and Lewis knew it. While the membership dropped from a peak 6,000,000 in 1945 to 4,300,000 in 1960, the wages of those miners who retained their jobs were still among the nation's highest.

When he announced his retirement in 1959 the mineowners presented him with an eighteenth-century set of Shakespeare in 15 volumes as a tribute to their most worthy opponent in the bitterest and hardest fought battles in American labor history. After his retirement Lewis was made President Emeritus of the United Mine Workers. In 1963 he retired as Chairman of the National Coal Policy Conference.

Whatever one thinks of Lewis' methods, manners, or motivations, his record speaks for itself. When he came to head the union in 1920 the average pay scale was $6.00 per day. When he retired it had risen to $24.25 daily. Members of his union are covered by some of the lushest sickness-accident and pension and welfare agreements in any industry in the nation. In 1920 they didn't receive so much as sick pay or vacations. Even his severest critics will concede that Lewis, more than any other man, brought about federal legislation making safety measures mandatory.

To just about everyone's surprise Lewis is truly retired in the sense that he does not meddle in union affairs and will not comment on strikes, contracts, or conditions in the coal or any other industry. He drives in from his Alexandria, Virginia, home every morning and busies himself with matters concerning the U.M.W.'s pension and welfare fund in the union's offices in Washington. His wife died in 1942. His son is a Washington, D. C., doctor; his daughter died a few years ago.

During a radio speech in 1936, and (right) in retirement today.

CBS   UPI

"RED" GRANGE

The only football player known to people who had never seen a game—nor cared to—was born in 1903, the son of the Chief of Police of Wheaton, Illinois. Playing for the local high school, he averaged five touchdowns a game. Although he had been offered scholarships from a score of colleges because of his record, when "Red" registered at the University of Illinois he was hesitant to join the team during his freshman year for fear of not being good enough. He was a genuine amateur athlete, and delivered ice in his hometown during summer vacations to earn spending money. He weighed around 170 pounds, and was 5 feet 11 inches. In an era of great heroes he became a living legend, later being elected to the Football Hall of Fame.

His real name was Harold Grange, but friends and fans referred to him as "Red" because of his shock of flaming red hair. The press had its own name for him: the "Galloping Ghost." He was the Touchdown King the way Babe Ruth was the Home-Run King. And like the Babe, Red had the kind of personality the sportswriters and public love to idolize. The greater his victory the more embarrassedly he seemed to discuss it, always going to great pains to mention the names of those who helped him during a game.

Notre Dame at the time had the Four Horsemen, but that was a group, and the twenties was a time of the individual in America. Until the advent of Red, college football was little more than a social event—boys and girls got to wear their coonskin coats, and the weather was an excuse to carry a hip flask full of bootleg booze. But now there was someone out on that field that people either loved or hated. The latter category was made up of all of those who did not root for the University of Illinois. The star system had come to football.

Sportswriters even today can't make up their minds which his best game was, a case of an embarrassment of riches. An idea of his playing can be gathered from the record of what for Grange was his worst year: In 1925 he went scoreless in four games out of seven. He gained 1,213 yards running and accounted for 119 yards by 15 passes.

Soon after graduation, in 1926 he played a series of exhibition games and was paid the colossal fee of $300,000 to star in a silent film called *One Minute to Play*. In 1927 he was signed by the now nonexistent New York Yankees, and after a year with them went with the Chicago Bears. Pro football was looked upon before Grange's time as something slightly more respectable than ladies' wrestling matches, and wasn't very popular until he played it. The average attendance for a pro game at the Polo Grounds in New York had been about 18,000. On December 6, 1925, a total of 73,651 spectators came out to see the New York Giants throttled 19–7 by Red and the Chicago Bears.

Although he played even better football during his pro years, Grange is best remembered for when he wore the Illinois blue jersey with his orange 77 on the back, since retired on the Illinois campus. When in the 1964–65 season Jim Grabowski broke Red's old record by ripping off 239 yards from scrimmage against the 212 yards that Grange had compiled during a legendary performance against Michigan, Arthur Daley of *The New York Times* wrote: "Bully for Grabowski. He put on a fine show last Saturday and is fully entitled to take bows. But whenever he encounters 'Red' Grange henceforth, he still should tip his hat." Paul Gallico called him "The Artful Dodger of the Century," and columnists linked him romantically with a string of beauties including Bebe Daniels and Clara Bow.

Grange had a few critics. One occasioned a classic remark—paraphrased many times since—when the Michigan campus newspaper placed Red on its second rather than first All-American list, he stated loftily: "All Grange can do is run." "And all *Galli-Curci* can do is sing," cracked Illinois coach Bob Zuppke. Galli-Curci was the great coloratura. After he retired from pro football in 1934 Red went into a job as sales manager for a bottling company, and then managed a nightclub in Hollywood for a while. In the late thirties he went into the insurance business as an agent. After a serious heart attack in the early 1950's, Red began to take things easy in the insurance business. After recuperating for a few seasons he did a television commentary of the Bears' games.

He had made a fortune during his pro years and invested it profitably. The last few years he has spent in semiretirement in his home in the Indian Lakes Estates of Florida. During the 1966–67 football season Falstaff Beer engaged him to do some commercials for them in the Midwestern markets.

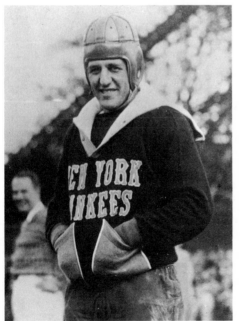

UPI

NBC

In 1927, during his one season with the New York Yankees, and today (*right*).

LIBBY HOLMAN

Her fans will tell you that no one ever sang the blues better than she. She introduced such standards as "Body and Soul," "Can't We Be Friends," and "Moanin' Low." That Libby had the right to sing the blues, no one would deny.

She was born Elizabeth Holzman in Cincinnati, Ohio, and first came to New York to get her law degree at Columbia University. Instead she made her Broadway debut in *Garrick Gaieties* in 1926.

Libby Holman was one of the brightest stars on Broadway, appearing in *The Little Show* (1929) and *Three's a Crowd* (1930), in which she introduced the song "Something to Remember You By," sung to a young man she selected from the band—Fred MacMurray, wearing a sailor suit, with his back to the audience. Then in 1932 her husband, Zachary Smith Reynolds, heir to a tobacco fortune estimated at $30,000,000, was killed. "Skipper" Reynolds, as he was called by his family and friends, was shot to death.

At first the coroner reported the death to be a suicide, but after Reynolds' tutor told the sheriff about Skipper's mood at the time he was supposed to have killed himself, the case was reopened, with the coroner holding an inquest.

Libby was indicted for murder in the first degree, which later was reduced to second degree. Throughout the entire affair Miss Holman conducted herself beautifully—she had been a law student before going on the stage, and her father, who was also her lawyer, was one of the most prominent attorneys in Ohio.

After a letter from the Reynolds family to the authorities asking that the case be dropped, Libby Holman was freed. No one was ever brought to trial, and to this day the shooting remains unsolved. During the years following the tragedy in 1932 Libby was very frugal with her public appearances. Her last Broadway show was *You'll Never Know* in 1938, with costar Rex O'Malley (now living in Manhattan not far from Miss Holman's town house in the East Sixties.) Also in the cast was Lupe Velez.

After leaving Broadway, Libby played summer stock in *Burlesque* (1939), *The Greeks Had a Word for It* (1940), *My Sister Eileen* (1941), and *Over 21* (1945).

In 1941 Libby married Ralph Holmes, an airman in the R.A.F., son of the stage actor, Taylor Holmes, and brother of actor Phillips Holmes. Phillips was killed during the war flying for the Canadian Air Force. After Ralph and Libby separated he died from an overdose of sleeping pills in 1945. After that she went into seclusion, except for sporadic singing engagements.

Libby's only child by Reynolds, a boy born two months after charges were dropped against her in the death of his father, was killed while climbing a mountain in California in 1950.

It was her meeting with her old accompanist, Gerald Cook, that induced her to begin performing again after a long hiatus though in 1958 she appeared in *Yerma,* a play about a wife who kills her husband. In 1966 she cut an album of her standards for a small record company. "Moanin' Low," "Can't We Be Friends?" and "Body and Soul" were on one side with a selection of folk songs on the other. These are the numbers she does with Cook when the spirit moves her in her one-woman show, "Blues, Ballads, and Sin Songs," which she has played in New York for limited runs and in little theatres up and down the East Coast as well as on television once, in Eindhoven, Holland, during a tour of Europe with her one-woman show.

Unfortunately, none of the magic that Broadway audiences saw during her heyday was ever captured for the screen. Miss Holman dismisses her fans' laments by saying that it was simply not the medium for her. The spell she created then is still, however, evident in her old 78's.

Miss Holman's official residence is shared with her husband, artist Louis Shanker, in a house she calls "Tree Tops" in Stamford, Connecticut.

With Rex O'Malley (*left*) and Clifton Webb in the Broadway show *You Never Know* (1938), and today.

Marcus Blechman

AMOS 'N' ANDY

The popularity of *Amos 'n' Andy* has no counterpart in television, movies, or the stage. Their tenure on radio was the longest, their salaries were the highest, and their impact on life in the United States from the late twenties through the forties was the greatest. Throughout their careers they were the undisputed Kings of Radio.

The original names of the couple were "Sam 'n' Henry," one of the many blackface acts playing the vaudeville circuits from the time they met in 1919 until they went on station WGN in Chicago in 1925. The program was only mildly successful at first, but began to pick up listeners as they started to add some of their famous characters. In 1926 they moved to station WMAQ, also in Chicago, and changed their names to "Amos 'n' Andy." On August 19, 1929, the National Broadcasting Company put them on from coast to coast. Their appeal was immediate and seemingly universal—they were popular on Park Avenue as well as in Harlem. They were referred to in speeches on the floor of the United States Senate, and "Silent Cal" Coolidge spoke out long enough to advise his staff that he was not to be disturbed while the show was on the air.

Amos, the working member of the team, was played by Freeman F. Gosden. He was supposed to run the Fresh Air Taxicab Company, consisting of one old car. His wife was Ruby, and they had a little girl, Arbadella. Andy, who had no job or business, was portrayed by Charles Correll. In spite of his lack of ambition he maintained an office and a secretary, Miss Blue.

Sponsored by the Pepsodent Tooth Paste Company, Amos 'n' Andy were heard Monday through Friday from 7:00 P.M. to 7:15 P.M. E.S.T. in every state in the Union, plus Canada. In some sections of the country theatre marquees announced that the feature film ended before 7 P.M. and did not begin again until after 7:15. Department stores that stayed open late some evenings broadcasted the shows on every floor, lest the patrons stay home for fear of missing an episode. When Andy was about to marry Madame Queen (which he never did) and when she brought a breach of promise suit against him, streets were deserted while America listened to "Brother Crawford," "Lightnin'," and "The Kingfish" testify.

Much of the show's activity centered around the Hall of the Mystic Knights of the Sea, the lodge to which all male members of the cast belonged. There was Lawyer Calhoon who conferred with his clients in the alley behind the jail, and Needle Nose Fletcher, and Sapphire Stevens, the Kingfish's wife. There were expressions which became a part of the American idiom: "Buzz me, Miss Blue," "Check and double-check," "I'se regusted!" and their famous lament, "Ow wah! Ow wah!" A foreigner walking down a typical American street during those years could hear the show's theme, "The Perfect Song," coming from every window on the block as though it had been piped in by government order.

In 1948 Gosden and Correll sold *Amos 'n' Andy* to CBS lock, stock and barrel, giving them an enormous tax break through capital gains and they continued to do the shows as employees of the network.

There was, however, a segment of the country that never found the characters amusing. After the war the rumblings of discontent among civil rights organizations protesting the stereotypes of Negroes the show created became more and more vocal. In the fifties the format was changed to permit guest stars, and the racial humor was toned down considerably. They were now on only once a week for 30 minutes in a program they called *The Amos 'n' Andy Music Hall,* and when Negro actors played the parts on the TV series (with Gosden and Correll keeping a hand in behind the scenes) it was hoped the complaints would cease, but if anything, the pressure grew.

Gosden and Correll discontinued the radio shows in 1958, and in 1965 CBS announced that the television series was being withdrawn from circulation, although the network denied the reason was protests from Negro organizations.

How the pair feels about being canceled after so many years of tremendous popularity can only be guessed at. They still maintain offices in Beverly Hills, but there are no announcements of future shows. When queried about their plans and opinions their answer is that they are still under contract to the Columbia Broadcasting System, and can make no further comment. The network's legal department refuses to confirm or deny that a contract exists, and the program department simply says that no program is scheduled for them in the foreseeable future.

Gosden and Correll are still the closest of friends, and play a lot of golf together in Palm Springs and on courses around Los Angeles. They were both married in 1927. Correll is an avid movie fan, and has flown his own plane for years. Gosden and he both enjoy fishing. In fact, the only time they ever missed a show was once in the thirties when they got so engrossed with a big catch they forgot the time, disappointing more Americans than ever voted for a Presidential candidate.

Amos (*left*) 'n' Andy in a scene from their movie *The Big Broadcast of 1936.*

(*From left to right*) Charles Correll (Andy), announcer Bill Hay, and Freeman F. Gosden (Amos) on a visit to the CBS studios in Hollywood. *CBS*

Testifying before a Senate committee in 1941 against Lend-Lease, and (below) today. *Wide World*

GERALD L. K. SMITH

When "Kingfish" Huey Long was assassinated in 1935, the man who took his place was a former Disciple of Christ minister who in 1933 had left his pulpit to become the Louisiana Senator's right-hand man. Gerald L. K. Smith delivered the eulogy at Long's funeral, and has continued over the years to carry on the Long tradition of fiery oratory and controversy.

Smith threw his "Share-the-Wealth" strength in with Father Coughlin and Dr. Townsend in 1936 to form the Union Party in an attempt to split the Democratic vote and thereby defeat Franklin D. Roosevelt in the Presidential election of that year. Smith still blames F.D.R. for many, if not most, of the ills of America and the world.

He was a strong and articulate opponent of Lend-Lease, and continued after his friend, Father Coughlin, was silenced to call for isolationism up to just before the attack on Pearl Harbor. His speeches were peppered with such phrases as "Let's keep America American," "America first" and "They want us to water the dry sticks of the earth with American blood and gold."

Until he moved his headquarters in the late forties from Detroit, Michigan, to Los Angeles he operated under the banner of the Committee of One Million.

Smith's major stock-in-trade for decades has consisted of raucous hate-mongering. Crude invective against the Jews, Negroes and other minority groups has made up much of his propaganda line.

In 1944 Smith ran for President on the America First party ticket, and again in 1956 he made the race under the banner of the Christian Nationalist Crusade. In 1952 he ran General Douglas MacArthur with no official nod from the General in a write-in campaign. The General was one of Smith's heroes along with Senator Joseph McCarthy and Henry Ford, Sr. When in 1956 Smith tried to associate himself with the Vice Presidential candidacy of Richard Nixon, his bid was met with a vigorous rebuff. "There is no place in the Republican Party," stated Mr. Nixon, "for the race-baiting merchandisers of hate like Gerald L. K. Smith."

Although Gerald L. K. Smith is as active as he ever was, unless one subscribes to *The Cross and the Flag*, the official organ of the Christian Nationalist Crusade, little is known of his statements and plans. Among his claims in this monthly magazine, which has a circulation of 40,000, is that it is a "big lie" or "pure fiction" that the Nazis murdered six million Jews in World War II.

Far from having mellowed with the years, his editorials warn America of emigration by national and ethnic groups of lower mental and physical capacities than those which Smith feels founded and developed the United States. He has supported Barry Goldwater for the Presidency, called for the impeachment of Chief Justice Earl Warren, and for the withdrawal of this country from the United Nations.

Throughout his public life Smith has been encouraged by his wife Elna, who often appears with him on the speaker's platform. It was in her name that in 1966 he constructed a huge concrete statue of Christ atop a 1,500-foot Ozark mountain in Eureka, Arkansas. Called Christ of the Ozarks, its height of 65 feet is over twice the size of the famous Christ of the Andes, and is built, says Smith, "to stand for 2,000 or 3,000 years."

Smith divides his time between Los Angeles and Tulsa, Oklahoma, maintaining homes and offices in each. His title is the National Director of the Christian Nationalist Crusade, which he describes as being "more or less the right-wing godfather and godmother to some 1,700 right-wing groups."

Summarizing its appraisal of Smith in 1948 in a report entitled "Subversive Activities of Hate Groups," the Americanism Commission, Department of Illinois of the American Legion, stated that "Gerald L. K. Smith is probably the most vicious of the rabble-rousing and sensational hate-mongers operating today."

Chase Photo, Ltd.

Mr. and Mrs. John Barrymore, 1939.

ELAINE BARRIE BARRYMORE

The Barrie-Barrymore affair has been rivaled only by the Liz Taylor-Richard Burton liaison of recent years. Miss Barrie and Barrymore, however, carried on for a much longer time, and had the Great Depression for the drab backdrop to their colorful capers.

It all began when Elaine Jacobs, a teenage student at Hunter College in New York City, left her home with her mother one day to see the greatest matinee idol of his day, John Barrymore, in the film, *Svengali*. She never really returned. From that day on Elaine called herself Elaine Barrie. It was that name that she signed to a note she sent to Barrymore who was undergoing one of his periodic alcohol cures in a hospital. The "interview" he granted was a long one, and was followed by another every day after that until he was discharged and moved into the Jacobs' family apartment on West End Avenue.

Barrymore's divorce from his second wife, actress Dolores Costello, was not yet final. Elaine was thirty years younger than he and still a minor. The press went wild. With Mrs. Jacobs in tow they were seen at nightclubs, theatres, and parties all around New York until he fled to Hollywood. Elaine was quick to follow and the tabloids reported every ridiculous detail. "Ariel and Caliban" was what the headlines dubbed them, and they pushed the New Deal right off the front pages.

In 1935 the Associated Press named Elaine Barrie and Republican Presidential Candidate Alf Landon as the two people who had made that year

48

most interesting. She was to make news for the next six years with their marriage and many separations until they were divorced shortly before his death in 1942.

The little girl who made up her mind to meet and marry John Barrymore succeeded in doing both. In the process she made a brief appearance in one of his films, costarred with him on Broadway, and acted with him in a number of radio dramas. By the time it ended, her mother, who had been with them most of the time, was divorced, Elaine's acting career was ruined, and Barrymore had become nearly as well known for his protégée as he had been for his profile.

Says Ariel about the Great Lover: "He made me unashamed of the natural. He made me glory in my sensuality. My head still whirls from the memories."

Barrymore's other wives were the writer Michael Strange, now deceased, and the beautiful Dolores Costello, who is living on a ranch in Fallbrook, California.

Although her mother and father were remarried, Elaine has remained Mrs. Barrymore. Over the years she has been involved in a number of endeavors. In the forties she took courses at a school for writers in California, but waited until 1964 to write her book, *All My Sins Remembered*. From 1950 until 1952 she was a customers' girl at a New York brokerage house.

In 1952 her father died, and Elaine and her mother went to Haiti for a week's vacation. They stayed nine years, and developed a very successful business of exporting straw baskets and handbags which are sold in such stores as Nieman-Marcus and Saks Fifth Avenue under the trade name of Elaine Barrymore Originals. Because of the political climate in Haiti they returned to New York in 1963.

In 1966 Elaine was engaged as a Special Consultant to the Alliance for Progress as a result of her firsthand knowledge of several South American nations.

That same year the Barrymore operation was moved to Trinidad, where mother and daughter now reside.

Now a businesswoman.

A young high school teacher in 1925, and (*below*) a geologist now, living quietly with his wife and two sons. *Culver Pictures*

JOHN T. SCOPES

When the General Assembly of the State of Tennessee passed a law forbidding the teaching of Darwin's theory of evolution in the public schools, John T. Scopes was a twenty-four-year-old mathematics teacher in the little town of Dayton. He was a soft-spoken young man who coached the football team and generally kept to himself. That was in the spring of 1925.

Shortly after the bill became law Scopes met with three lawyers in Robinson's Drugstore, and over a few bottles of soda pop decided to become the key figure in one of the world's most famous trials. It was a matter of conviction on the part of the freckled young man, for he shied away from publicity, and even during the heat of the controversy managed to keep in the background as much as possible.

A few days after he made up his mind to test the law in the courts, Scopes deliberately read to his students a portion of Hunter's *Civic Biology* which stated that man has descended from a lower form of mammal. He was indicted, and a trial was set for July, 1925.

By the time the proceedings got under way Dayton had been swollen to nearly three times its normal size of 1,500. It was a sleepy little country town nestled in the foothills of the Cumberland Mountains. From all over the world there came reporters, sightseers, souvenir hawkers, telegraph operators, and some of the finest legal minds in America. It was to be immortalized in history books, plays, motion pictures, and newspapers as the setting for the "Monkey Trial," or as some referred to it, the "Trial of the Century."

Scopes was prosecuted by three-time Democratic Presidential candidate, William Jennings Bryan, who had also been a United States Secretary of State and one of this country's most colorful orators. He was defended by Clarence Darrow, the most famous criminal lawyer in America, fresh from his triumph in the Loeb-Leopold case in Chicago. Assisting Darrow were Arthur Garfield Hays and Dudley Field Malone, highly respected attorneys in their own rights. But even with such a team on the defense the deck was stacked against Scopes. Dayton was what H. L. Mencken, who covered the trial with great glee for the *Baltimore Sun*, called "the buckle on the Bible Belt."

The heat was so great that Judge John T. Raulston moved the trial out onto the shaded lawn, which lowered the temperature somewhat but did not affect the heated insults a bit. Bryan announced that he had come to "defend the word of God against the greatest atheist and agnostic in the world today." He meant Darrow, who in turn called the aging "Great Commoner" to the stand as a witness for the defense, humiliating him by making his religious beliefs seem ludicrous.

Theoretically Bryan won. Scopes was found guilty and fined $100, which the *Baltimore Sun* offered to pay. But the press had laughed at Bryan, and even the crowd in the courtroom had become disappointed as he floundered foolishly on the witness stand under Darrow's barrage of cutting questions. In less than a week the "Defender of the Word," as he liked to be called, died of an apoplectic stroke.

Darrow announced that his client would not pay the fine, and that the case would be appealed. The higher court found that the judge had erred in setting the sentence rather than permitting the jury to do so.

In the years that followed Scopes avoided the limelight like a plague. He left Dayton the day the trial ended, and the only time reporters had a real opportunity with him was in 1943 when he turned up in Kentucky and announced that he would run for the United States Congress on the Socialist party ticket. But he would discuss only the campaign issues. He was defeated as expected. He did not return to Dayton again until 1960, when the town that had scorned him as an "infidel" thirty-five years before feted him on the occasion of the world premiere of the film, *Inherit the Wind*— adapted from the successful Broadway stage play dramatizing the trial. (Scopes was played by actor Dick York and, like all the real characters in the picture, was given a fictitious name.)

Once the world's most famous schoolteacher, John T. Scopes now lives and works quietly in Shreveport, Louisiana, as an executive for an oil and gas company, taking time out to write his memoirs. He says it has been a long time since he has received one of those letters asking him if he believes that his grandmother was an ape. When asked if he would do it all over again, he replied that perhaps someone should because that same law is still on the books of Tennessee.

Wide World

In 1936, a ranking Republican Congress-man, and powerful adversary of Roosevelt foreign policy.

HAMILTON FISH

Had he done nothing from 1920 to 1945 in the House of Representatives but show up for roll calls, Hamilton Fish would be immortal because of the 1940 speech made by President Roosevelt which ended with the famous words, "Martin, Barton, and Fish."

After leaving Harvard in 1910 he went to France as an officer with the famous 369th Infantry where he and his men (all of them Negroes, with the exception of the officers) fought in the Battle of Champagne. At the end of World War I Fish was a Major, he had been decorated with the *croix de guerre,* and his outfit had one of the finest fighting records in the United States forces. It was at this time that he entered politics.

Even as a freshman, Congressman Fish took the lead. He proposed legislation for the establishment of the Tomb of the Unknown Soldier, and during the twenties, when the Negro Civil Rights bandwagon was offering "immediate seating," Fish introduced countless bills to guarantee equality for the men who fought alongside him so valiantly during the war. Far from being the conservative he was later thought to be, he fought for prison reform, and recommended that the three who figured prominently in the Teapot Dome Scandal, Fall, Doheney, and Sinclair—all millionaires—be sent to prison. One of the founders of the American Legion, Fish defended the veterans' bonus at a time when many on his side of the aisle were firmly set against it.

In 1930 he formed the Fish Committee, which was the precursor of the Dies Committee, but his attempts to unearth Communists were unsuccessful. He continued, however, as one of the first well-known politicians to make communism an issue, and in 1931 asked that the Communist party in the United States be outlawed. His first big break with Roosevelt came in 1933 when the new President recognized the Soviet Union. He did support many of the New Deal economic measures because he felt they were necessary under the circumstances of the Depression. But he was vehemently opposed to America's interference in European politics.

By the late thirties, when World War II seemed a probability, Fish through seniority had become the ranking Republican on the House Rules

Committee and the Foreign Affairs Committee, two of the most powerful groups in the federal government. By this time Fish was making speeches for groups such as America First and the Liberty League, warning the American people that the powers Roosevelt was asking for were those of a war President. He fought the President on the floor and in the cloakroom of the House on such measures as lend-lease and the draft, and campaigned vigorously against the repeal of the arms embargo. The powerful National Committee to Keep America Out of Foreign Wars, an isolationist movement that got under way in 1939, was a Fish brainchild.

When Pearl Harbor was attacked, one of the first voices heard was that of Hamilton Fish in support of President Roosevelt.

When Fish ran each time for office it was from the district that included F.D.R.'s ancestral home, Hyde Park. Try as he did to unseat Fish, the congressman returned to office each year until the district was gerrymandered in 1945. Confronted with a new electorate, he was at last retired by the voters. Since 1945 Fish has been active in speaking before various patriotic groups, campaigning for candidates of his political persuasion, and as President General of the Order of Lafayette (an organization of such eminent citizens as Admiral Chester Nimitz, General Omar Bradley, former Postmaster General James A. Farley, and former French Ambassador Hervé Alphand).

Since the death of Mrs. Fish several years ago he has lived in a midtown New York City hotel near the Harvard Club, of which he is a member. He can now laugh about his heated disputes with F.D.R. but has lost none of his old vigor when defending his old stands. About Roosevelt, he says: "He had great personal charm. An excellent public speaker, but he was a small man. Small in his outlook and petty in his anger. He lied us into that war. It was a low and despicable thing to do. What he wanted was power."

About the famous speech which had the nation howling, Fish remarks: "I was very pleased, actually. Those other two—Barton and Martin—two fine men. I considered myself in good company. Of course, it was funny. Roosevelt knew just how to time it so it would be funny. What historians neglect to mention is that he didn't write the speech. He didn't write any of his speeches."

At the Harvard Club in New York City recently. *John P. Gilligan*

In her 1935 stage debut in the United States, starring in *Escape Me Never*. *Vandamm*

ELISABETH BERGNER

The famous actress, who had her training at the equally famous Vienna Conservatory, made her first success in 1921 opposite one of the most renowned actors of the time, Alexander Moissi, as Ophelia to his Hamlet.

Almost immediately Elisabeth Bergner was one of the biggest stars in Germany and her native Austria. The legendary Max Reinhardt guided her in a number of Shakespearean plays in the twenties, and she was also to be seen in *A Doll's House* and *Miss Julie*.

Her husband, Dr. Paul Czinner, directed her in a number of silent films beginning in 1924. In *Nju* and *Violinist of Florence* she costarred with the late Conrad Veidt. The latter film as well as *Donna Juanna* were released through U.F.A., the MGM of Germany, and produced by her own firm known as the Elisabeth Bergner Poetic Film Company.

With her triumph in *St. Joan* on stage in 1924 the Bergner reputation was sufficient to warrant a tour of Holland, Sweden, and Denmark. In 1926 she essayed the title role in a popular play of the time, *The Last of Mrs. Cheyney*. For the 1930–31 seasons in Germany and Austria she appeared under Reinhardt's auspices in Eugene O'Neill's *Strange Interlude*. During 1932 she made the films *Der Traumende* and *Ariane* in Paris.

The hit of West End's season in 1933 was Elisabeth Bergner in *Escape Me Never*. She played an enchanting and gallant gamine named Gemma Jones. The bobbed blond hair and shorts she wore in the play in England and on Broadway (1935) and in the film set fashion trends.

Another style set by Elisabeth Bergner was the bare midriff, which she introduced in her 1937 movie *Dreaming Lips*.

After Hitler came to power in Germany and Austria all of the star's appearances were either in England or America. The films she made in England were well received in the United States. But those big, brown, pleading eyes were in all too few motion pictures. Even in a poor one such as *Catherine the Great* (1934) her performance was outstanding. Her leading man in *As You Like It* (1937) was the promising young actor Laurence Olivier, and in *Stolen Life* (1939) her leading man was Michael Redgrave. In 1943 Bergner was once again charming Broadway audiences in the chiller *The Two Mrs. Carrolls*. She toured Australia in it in 1950.

In England and on the Continent, the Viennese actress has through the years appeared in such plays as *The Boy David*, playing the title role (this was Sir James Barrie's last play), Terence Rattigan's *The Deep Blue Sea* in which she toured Germany and Austria in 1954, and *Long Day's Journey into Night* at the 1959 Berlin Festival. On another tour abroad during the late fifties she did *Dear Liar*, the dramatization of the George Bernard Shaw-Mrs. Patrick Campbell correspondence.

She did not appear in this country again until she accepted the mother role in *First Love*, a play for the 1961–62 season from the book by Romain Gary. Unfortunately while the company was in out-of-town tryouts Miss Bergner and director Alfred Lunt agreed that the "difficulties" were too great. She withdrew and was replaced.

The lady, whom Alexander Woollcott praised as "probably the ablest actress in the world today," makes her home in London. She and Dr. Czinner have been married over forty years.

Miss Bergner now lives quietly in London.

CHRISTINE JORGENSEN

On more than one occasion the Presidential election campaigns of 1952 were bumped from the front pages of United States newspapers with revelations concerning a former G.I. named George Jorgensen, Jr., who had gone to Denmark and had been changed into a woman.

Born in New York City in 1926, Jorgensen, who was an only child, had felt an overwhelming desire through school, the Army, and various jobs, to look, act, sound, and dress feminine. While groping in every direction toward some answer to the obsession that alienated him from every group, he came across a book entitled *The Male Hormone*. Shortly after reading it he sailed in 1950 for Denmark on the pretext of making a color travel film on the country.

During 1950, 1951, and early 1952 Danish doctors performed a series of operations, and treated George with hormones. In June of 1952 he wrote to his parents in the Bronx informing them of the fact that he would be coming back to America shortly—as Miss Christine Jorgensen. Mr. and Mrs. Jorgensen, who had always been aware of how deeply troubled their boy was, took it quite well. Several months later the story broke all over the world. What seemed a welcome, if somewhat bizarre, answer to a great problem changed into a nightmare as their home was turned into a circus by newspaper reporters and the plain curious.

Christine arrived back in this country and stated that, contrary to reports, she was not going to star in a Hollywood movie. She said her career was behind the camera, not in front of it: "I am a photographer, not an actress." Miss Jorgensen insisted that she did not want any publicity. She insisted on it during newspaper and magazine interviews, on TV and radio shows, and in her life story which was published in a national magazine.

The former soldier who turned lady for a lifetime took an apartment in Manhattan's Gramercy Park area, and was seen at openings and parties around town for several years. The travel films were somehow forgotten and she was seriously considered by a Hollywood producer for the title role in the remake of *She,* but nothing came of it. After interest in her bizarre story waned she submitted to one of Mike Wallace's grueling personal TV interrogations. A small company put out an LP record album of an interview with her. Although in sales it fell somewhat short of the Top 40, it is today something of a classic in recorded bad taste, and a much-sought-after collector's item among discophiles.

Miss Jorgensen has twice taken out a marriage license but has yet to marry because she "simply wasn't in love." She feels that many women over thirty-five make the mistake of marrying just because they are embarrassed to be single at that age. Although she thinks she may never marry, she does not rule out the possibility. To the question of whether or not marriage for Christine is legally possible she points out that the United States State Department in 1952 changed her passport, thus making her gender legally female.

As her name began to appear less and less in the columns, and comics found new personalities to joke about, Christine began to do summer stock and nightclubs. She has played Madame Rosepetal in *Oh Dad, Poor Dad, Mamma's Hung You in the Closet and I'm Feelin' So Sad, Tom Jones,* and the title role in *Mary, Mary* on the strawhat circuit during 1963, 1964, and 1965. In 1966 she took her nightclub act, in which she sings a little, tells jokes, and answers questions from the audience, to Hawaii.

Between engagements Miss Jorgensen is kept busy answering letters that still pour in from around the world, written by young men and women who are unhappy with their gender. Although she maintains she has never had the slightest regret about changing her sex, the advice she gives them is to seek psychiatric and medical help before undergoing surgery. According to Christine, sex changes are not at all uncommon in the United States. She claims that one took place recently in the hospital of a United States prison and another on a United States naval base.

She says that she has many friends who are homosexuals, but that she was never one herself in the usual sense of the word. In fact, she maintains that she really doesn't understand the problem in others.

Her parents moved to Massapequa, Long Island, in 1953, and when her father died a number of months ago Christine began living with her surviving parent. When told about this recently, the writer Dorothy Parker quipped, "And what sex, may I ask, is the mother?"

Among her plans for the future is her long-awaited autobiography, which she is working on now. Those who expect to find it full of glimpses into her sex life and transvestite humor will be greatly disappointed. Miss Christine Jorgensen thinks of herself as a lady in every sense of the word, and takes the whole thing very seriously.

George before leaving for Denmark, 1949 (*left*).

Now Christine, portraying Madam Rosepetal in *Oh Dad, Poor Dad, Momma's Hung You in the Closet and I'm Feelin' So Sad.*

Counsel to millions on *The Goodwill Hour,* at the height of his popularity, 1939.

JOHN J. ANTHONY

The little man who gave advice to tens of thousands during his career was for a time so successful that his radio shows were carried by two networks at the same time.

His famous phrases, "No names, please." and "What is your problem, Madam?" became known to all. John J. Anthony was a household word. "Tell it to the Marines" was replaced by "Tell it to Mr. Anthony."

Mr. Anthony, or "Mr. Agony" as many called him, got the idea for his radio program in jail. He had been given a three-month sentence for failing to pay alimony to his first wife for the support of their two sons. After that he served another shorter sentence, and twice was cited for contempt of court—all because he didn't believe in alimony.

In those days he went under his real name, Lester Kroll. He went to jail in New York City as a cab driver. He emerged as the head of an organization he created and called "The Alimony League," a movement he was later to use in lobbying against many of the archaic marriage and divorce laws on the state's books.

He began his broadcasts on April 10, 1930. The show would open with his announcer, the distinguished actor Roland Winters, saying: "You have a friend and adviser in John J. Anthony. And thousands are happier and more successful today *because* of John J. Anthony!"

Mr. Anthony never permitted his guests to mention names (only initials were used), religion, or to give too many details. If at all possible, the suggestion of sex crept into the conversation. Though never blatant, if there was a way to titillate the audience without offense it was done.

Although a great many who listened to him during his more than twenty-five years on network radio did not take him seriously, he claims a good deal of the credit for making premarital blood tests mandatory in many states, and the establishment of the three-day waiting period between the granting of a license and the marriage ceremony. John J. Anthony's peak of popularity was at a time in this country when a great many Americans were hungry and depressed. The sorrows interviewees poured out to the little man on the radio, perhaps made them forget their own problems. Whatever the reasons for people listening and people confessing, he has never had a single complaint from anyone he advised.

Mr. Anthony, author of a book, *Marriage and Family Problems*, which sold over 400,000 copies, is now living in Los Angeles. After his network shows were cancelled in the mid-fifties he had for a time a local radio program and TV show. Now all of his time is spent as a Commissioner of Human Relations for the County of Los Angeles. To this day he is in touch with people who came to him seeking his advice many years ago.

When asked about his own family life he said, "I have been married to the same woman now for over thirty years. I think I must be in a rut."

Entering a sound stage for his appearance in the recent movie *Divorce, American Style*, with Debbie Reynolds and Dick Van Dyke.

Circa 1935.

CHARLES ATLAS

Body-builder Angelo Siciliano migrated in 1904 along with his family to Brooklyn from the farm in Acri, Italy, where he was born. Angelo was a weak, sickly boy, listless and unhappy. One night, when he was fifteen years old, while returning home he was attacked and beaten severely by a bigger boy. It must have hurt an awful lot because he has never forgotten it—nor has the public.

The 97-pound teenager brooded over the incident, and then after being impressed with a statue of Hercules set about exercising at the local gymnasiums. The more he lifted weights the more tired he got. While visiting the zoo one day Angelo, impressed with the lion's muscles, wondered how it could be so powerful with no room to exercise in that small cage. While staring at the animal, it got up and stretched. Seeing the beast pit one muscle against the other gave the boy the idea for what was to change his life and the lives of many others around the world. It was the basis for the system he called "Dynamic Tension."

Employing the principles he worked out on himself, he won a national contest in 1922, conducted by Bernarr Macfadden, to name the "World's Most Perfectly Developed Man." When he again won the following year, MacFadden in disgust retired the title.

Someone remarked how much he looked like the statue of Atlas that stood on the site of a local bank. It flattered the young man, who at the time was working as a $5-a-week strong man and janitor for a Coney Island sideshow. He decided to change his name to Charles Atlas.

In the early 1920's a friend got him a job as a life model. Within a short time he was in demand and earning $100 a week allowing people to admire and to draw his body. But if they liked it so much, why not show them how such a physique can be theirs—for profit? In 1929 he began a correspondence course which had only mild success until a young man from an advertising firm, Charles P. Roman, gave him some ideas for promotion.

In 1942 Atlas publicized his system by pulling six cars chained together for a full mile while the public and the press looked on in awe. Another time he towed a 72½-ton railroad car 112 feet along the tracks with a rope. His imaginative advertising ran in comic books, Sunday supplements, and just about every type of magazine that a man was likely to pick up. It was presented in a series of simple drawings any male could understand and identify with. The situation is set on a beach. A puny man's girl is taken away from him, and sand is kicked in his face by a bully. If that puny guy were you, the easy thing to do was to send for the free illustrated booklet which encouraged you to sign up. Around the world, millions did.

Atlas takes his body building method seriously and with good reason—it works. Most of the principles of the "new" isometrics are based on exercises that Atlas pioneered thirty years ago. He is most proud of some of his famous pupils, Fred Allen, Max Baer, and Mahatma Gandhi.

Charles Roman, who gave Atlas the idea for promoting himself and his system, still runs the mail-order business. The ads are very much the same, and the symbolism is as always a photograph of Charles Atlas in the classic Atlas pose with the globe resting on his back.

Atlas gave up his gymnasium in New York several years ago. He visits his offices in London, and when traveling within the United States flies in a twin-engine plane piloted by Charles Roman.

When he is in town the paunchy businessmen at the New York Athletic Club stare in wonderment at the physique of the man in his sixties working out in the gym.

Some years ago Charles Atlas moved near an abandoned Coast Guard lookout station on Point Lookout, Long Island. Here he spends most of his time. He has made his house a most unusual one, furnishing it with furniture he built himself from the driftwood that floats up on the shore.

Mrs. Atlas, to whom he was married for forty years, died in 1965, leaving a son and a daughter.

Today, a little gray and a different bathing suit.

At the peak of his popularity, 1943. From the smile on his face it is a safe guess that there was good news that night. *Mutual Network*

GABRIEL HEATTER

During the Second World War, despite his "Voice of Doom" delivery, his famous "Ah, yes, there's *good* news tonight" lightened the worries of many who had boys in the service.

In 1909 when William Randolph Hearst, the late publisher, was running for the office of Mayor in New York, he hired a teenager from the Lower East Side named Gabriel Heatter to precede him at rallies as a boy orator, a fad at the time among evangelists and politicians. Hearst lost the election, but the young man worked for his paper, the *American*, and several others as a messenger and cub reporter until he made the grade as a full reporter. By the end of the First World War he had done well enough in the newspaper business to become the representative in Paris for several American papers.

By 1930, back in New York, his debates on Socialism with Norman Thomas, which were published in *The Nation*, had made him a name among his colleagues. The press if not the public was aware of Heatter.

Gabriel Heatter was propelled into national prominence when in 1936 he reported over the radio the electrocution of Bruno Richard Hauptmann, the kidnapper of the Lindbergh baby. Something went wrong with the apparatus that circulated the electricity into the electric chair in New Jersey's death house. Caught with no script, no preparation, and no warning, Heatter did an amazing 53-minute ad lib giving listeners across the nation the background of the crime, the trial, and the last-minute legal maneuvers. His colorful descriptions of the prison, death chamber, and atmosphere that prevailed that night held audiences spellbound until the execution was finally able to proceed.

62

This was at a time when radio was really beginning to come into its own as a news medium. The press considered it a bastard form of reporting and treated it with contempt when they mentioned it at all. The Heatter-Hauptmann scoop did not help make friends between the two media, nor did it endear him personally to the newspapers.

The events in Europe as the raging of Hitler sounded across the Atlantic made the public all the more anxious to get their news right away. Heatter, along with the many other reporters in radio news, emerged as a personal contact between Americans and history as it was being made. Heatter's extremely personal delivery made him seem like a family friend—one whose word was to be trusted, counted on, and waited for eagerly each day.

His salary was for a while as high as $3,500 weekly. His Monday through Friday 15-minute newscasts around the dinner hour were carried by a 450-station hookup over the Mutual Network. Although his folksy approach made him the brunt of many jokes during those years, his popularity was every bit as great as that of his contemporaries, Lowell Thomas and Graham McNamee. For special events such as political conventions and famous trials he was Mutual's man-on-the-spot. During his network days he also did remote broadcasts from a coal mine, the roof of a skyscraper, and an airplane in flight. Heatter's distinctive voice was also familiar to newsreel audiences during the late thirties and forties as he narrated the events of the day.

Gabriel Heatter at seventy years old gave up his network program when he moved to Miami Beach in 1960. For a while he kept busy with broadcasts heard in Florida over WIOD. Of late, however, his health is the cause for giving up broadcasting, and he is concentrating all of his efforts on getting well. Gabriel lives with his wife, Sadie, in Miami Beach. He lists his hobbies as "fishing, reading, and martinis."

On a new station, WIOD, these days in Miami Beach, Florida.

He was "Black Lightning" when he reached the 1936 Olympic Games in Berlin. *UPI*

JESSE OWENS

The man who is generally regarded as being the greatest Negro athlete of all time was born on an Alabama tenant farm in 1913. One of seven children, Jesse moved with his family to Cleveland when he was quite young. His real name is James Cleveland Owens, and after he took to calling himself "J.C." his schoolmates and family soon made it "Jesse."

In junior high school he established a new record by making the 100-yard dash in 10 seconds flat. At the 1933 National Interscholastic Championships at the University of Chicago everyone sat up and took notice when he made the 100 yards in 9.4 seconds, the 200 yards in 20.7 seconds, and a broad jump of 24 feet 9⅝ inches.

During his freshman year at Ohio State University he worked as a gas station attendant until a Negro member of the Ohio Legislature had him put on as a page in the House of Representatives in the State's capitol.

He began earning names such as "Brown Bombshell" and "Buckeye Bullet" when in 1935 he broke three world records and tied for a fourth at the National Collegiate track and field Championships held at the University of Michigan. In what *The New York Times* has described as "the greatest day in the history of track" he made a 100-yard dash in 9.4 seconds, a 220-yard dash in 20.3 seconds, a 220-yard low hurdle in 22.6 seconds, and a broad jump of 25 feet 9 inches. He did it all on May 25, 1935.

"Owens was so matchless in sheer grace and speed," wrote Arthur Daley of the *Times* after observing the Negro at the 1936 Olympic Games, "that his like may never be seen again." Propaganda Minister Joseph Paul Goebbels, however, referred to him as "black American auxiliary." As though in defiance of Hitler's remarks before the games, about Aryan superiority, Owens established new world records: the 100-metre run (10³⁄₁₀ seconds), the 200-metre run (20⁷⁄₁₀ seconds), and the broad jump (25 feet 9²⁷⁄₃₂ inches). He came away with four gold medals and the friendship of Lutz Long, the German athlete who finished second. Ignoring Hitler's remarks about the Negro race, Lutz walked across the field with his arm around Owens' shoulder in full view of the Führer.

In 1936 Owens received an A.B. degree from Ohio State and announced that he was going to become a performer, whereupon he joined Bill "Bojangles" Robinson in a tap dancing act. That same year he supported Alf Landon for the Presidency and bought his parents an 11-room house in Cleveland.

From 1937 to 1939 he appeared around the country with his own swing band, served as an official of the WPA, and won a sprint against a race horse in Havana. At the end of 1939 several of the businesses he owned had failed and he declared bankruptcy.

From 1940 to 1942 he was with the Office of Civilian Defense in Philadelphia. Then he was in charge of Negro personnel during the war at the Ford Motor Car Company in Detroit. After the war he sold sporting goods, and was part owner of an all-Negro baseball team. In 1950 a national poll of sportswriters named him "the world's top track performer since 1900." Jim Thorpe came in second. In 1955 he made a tour of India for the State Department, which was considered an enormous success. He also appeared in European capitals as an emcee during the Harlem Globetrotter exhibitions put on by the famous Negro basketball team.

Owens is not rich today, and says he has no desire to be so again. He is the proprietor of a public relations firm that specializes in promoting Negro products, and he is heard over a Chicago radio station as a disc jockey. He lives comfortably with his wife, to whom he has been married since 1931. They have three daughters. The athlete, who was the first American to jump over 20 feet, is a member of the Illinois Youth Commission, and has stated that it is his belief that if children of any race, any economic class, are keenly interested in sports they won't have the time or energy for delinquency.

In 1966 Owens paid a $3,000 fine to the Federal Government for evading $68,166 in income tax. He said he felt the court had been very fair, considering the offense carries with it a maximum of four years in prison and a $40,000 fine.

Army football coach Paul Dietzel gets an autograph at a recent convention of the NCAA in Chicago. *UPI*

In a publicity picture
for NBC Radio in 1935.

JESSICA DRAGONETTE

There is no popular singer either in television or movies today who could be compared with Jessica Dragonette. At her peak she was singing to 66,000,000 Americans weekly. She commanded a loyalty from her fans equal to that of the late Jeanette MacDonald. When she left NBC in the late thirties after a disagreement with her sponsors over the format of her programs, her admirers threatened to boycott not only the product but radio itself until she returned. She was quickly snapped up by the rival network, CBS.

Jessica was born in India and brought to this country at an early age. She was still a little girl when she was orphaned and put in the care of nuns at a convent. As the Angel Voice in the New York stage play *The Miracle* she attracted the enthusiastic praise of the great Russian opera singer Boris Chaliapin.

Truly a broadcasting pioneer, Miss Dragonette appeared on one of the first telecasts in history, February 5, 1928, which was designed to evaluate the new medium. She was among the array of stars heard on the first broadcast from the new NBC studios when they opened in Radio City on November 11, 1932. She has appeared on radio for Palmolive Soap, Pet Milk, Ford Motor Company, Cities Service, and others.

No radio star did more for the war effort during the forties than Jessica Dragonette. Her countless appearances at War Bond rallies and tours of bases and camps entertaining troops brought her the United States Treasury Silver Medal and Wings from both the Army and Navy. She holds the rank of honorary colonel in the United States Air Force.

Jessica's one appearance in a motion picture, *The Big Broadcast of 1936,* was a segment made at the Paramount Studios in New York.

Her career on the concert stage was extremely successful—150,000 people turned out to hear her in Chicago's Grant Park; and in Minneapolis, in spite of a blizzard and taxi strike, she drew 15,000 at one performance; at the Potomac Water Gate in Washington, D.C., an overflow crowd of 18,000 heard her; at New York's Lewisohn Stadium, she appeared with the Philharmonic Symphony Orchestra before an audience of 22,000.

Jessica wrote her autobiography in 1952, *Faith Is a Song,* in which she explained in great detail the misunderstanding between her and the National Broadcasting Company. Until its publication the details had been one of the most widely speculated-about events in radio.

Because of her refusal throughout her career to allow her personal life to be publicized she became known in the columns as "The Garbo of Radio." Coincidentally, she has maintained a long friendship with the mysterious Greta Garbo, who lives close by in Manhattan.

In 1952, for her promotion of Spanish music, the Spanish Ambassador to the United States presented her with the medal of the Knot of the Order of Isabella the Catholic. A devout Roman Catholic all her life, Miss Dragonette was invested as Lady of Grand Cross of the Equestrian Order of the Holy Sepulchre of Jerusalem and awarded the Pro Pontifice et Ecclesia Cross from the Vatican.

She is the wife of Nicolas Turner, a New York businessman. They live on Manhattan's East 57th Street just a few doors from two of her contemporaries, Lanny Ross and Lucy Monroe. Jessica's friends are as varied as was her repertoire. A few of the most prominent guests who attend her parties are: former President Harry Truman, William Buckley, Jr., Jack Benny, Lily Pons, and Bishop Fulton J. Sheen.

Although Jessica tells interviewers that she has never given up her singing career, her concerts are certainly unknown to her many fans who still have vivid memories of the lady who was at one time known as "The Jenny Lind of the Air."

As she looks today.

At the microphone for his call, with Russ Morgan, in a 1941 broadcast. *CBS Radio*

JOHNNY

Johnny Roventini, the world's most famous midget, was born of Italian immigrant parents who, like his brothers and sisters, are of normal size. The exact year, according to Johnny, is a "midgetary secret."

Johnny was working as a page boy in the Hotel New Yorker during the Depression when the President of Philip Morris and the advertising man, Milton Biow, sent him on a fool's errand through the hotel's lobby calling for a man named Philip Morris. No one took that call, but the Philip Morris Company took Johnny and made him into one of the world's few living trademarks.

Johnny's perfect B-flat "Call for Philip Morris" backed by Ferde Grofé's "Grand Canyon Suite" (the popular "On the Trail" portion) was first heard on radio on April 17, 1933. The program featured baritone Ronny Weeks. The opening to each Philip Morris program was "Johnny presents . . . ," as when Johnny presented "Great Moments from Great Plays," "The Philip Morris Frolics," and one of the great dramatic shows from radio's golden days, "The Philip Morris Playhouse." Throughout the years in magazines, newspapers, cigarette cartons, and on TV and radio Johnny became the most recognized and valuable advertising gimmick in the country.

By his own conservative estimate, he has shaken the hands of close to a million people during his years for Philip Morris.

During World War II Johnny volunteered for both the Navy and the Coast Guard, but was repeatedly rejected because of his size. He even invited the commander of one recruiting district aboard the EVA-R, his cruiser, to demonstrate his facility as a sailor.

Johnny's radio career, the medium he still misses, was during the era of the big bands. A few with whom he appeared are: Ray Bloch, Harry James, Johnny Green, Jerry Gray, Russ Morgan, and Leo Reisman.

Some of the radio and television programs on which Johnny appeared are: *Life With Lucy, This Is Your Life, The Rudy Vallee Show, Candid Microphone* (forerunner of *Candid Camera*), *The Philip Morris Playhouse, Break the Bank, Crime Doctor,* Walter Kiernan's *One Man's Opinion, The Kate Smith Show, It Pays to Be Ignorant,* and *Casey, Crime Photographer.*

Over the years he has done a great deal of traveling for his sponsor. Wherever he goes he is invariably asked to give his call, which he has learned to deliver in Spanish, French, German, Swedish, Italian, and Chinese.

Although the Philip Morris Company ceased using both Johnny's picture and presence in their advertising and promotions during the early fifties, he is still under lifetime contract to them, and appears around the country at company sales meetings, conventions, and parties.

Johnny has never married and lives in Brooklyn with his sister in a house full of furniture and clothes scaled down to suit his 50-inch height. Since signing with the cigarette company Johnny has grown over an inch, a common occurrence among adult midgets. His employers still carry a huge insurance policy on his life, and pay the salary of his brother who acts as chauffeur and bodyguard. The famous midget drives about in a Sunbeam Alpine, plays lots of golf, and pilots his own 26-foot cruiser in Sheepshead Bay, Brooklyn.

Although he never appears in public without his little bellboy's uniform, Johnny has been caught off duty smoking a brand of cigarettes other than Philip Morris—his close friends will tell you he favors Marlboro (a Philip Morris product).

In a recent visit to his sponsor's office on Park Avenue. *Edward Oleksak*

In 1943, weighing in on opening day at Belmont Park. *UPI*

EDDIE ARCARO

Horse racing's richest, most famous jockey was born in Cincinnati, Ohio, in 1916. He left school after the ninth grade and has been racing horses ever since.

The expression "riding a winner" can be reversed to describe the career of Eddie Arcaro—more often than not it was a case of a horse being ridden by a winner. His incredible skill on the track with horses not ordinarily expected to come into the money decreased the track odds on whatever animal he rode.

His ability and luck began to show at seventeen, when he won on a gelding named No More at Washington Park in Chicago in 1935, and two years later in his first Kentucky Derby he came in fourth on the Calumet Farms horse Nellie Flag.

Although Arcaro has been six times a top money winner of the year, he was never counted among those jockeys with the most victories because he was always discriminating about what he rode and where rather than with how many. A glance at his record indicates his good judgment:

KENTUCKY DERBY (Churchill Downs)

Year	Horse	Purse
1938	Lawrin	$47,050
1941	Whirlaway	61,275
1945	Hoop, Jr.	64,850
1948	Citation	83,400
1952	Hill Gail	96,300

BELMONT STAKES (Belmont Park)

Year	Horse	Purse
1941	Whirlaway	39,770
1942	Shut Out	44,520
1945	Pavot	52,675
1948	Citation	77,700
1952	One Count	82,400
1955	Nashua	83,700

PREAKNESS STAKES (Pimlico)

1941	Whirlaway	49,365
1948	Citation	91,870
1950	Hill Prince	56,110
1951	Bold	83,100
1955	Nashua	67,550
1957	Bold Ruler	65,250

Arcaro, Johnny Longden, and Sir Gordon Richards are the only three jockeys ever to ride over 4,000 winners. He is twice winner of racing's Triple Crown (Kentucky Derby, Preakness, and the Belmont Stakes), in 1941 on Whirlaway and in 1948 on Citation. In 1955, on Nashua, he lost to Swaps by a length and a half in the Kentucky Derby, but in a special match race later for $100,000 he won by six and a half lengths.

Arcaro has ridden and won for stakes well over $23,000,000 during his career, which ended in 1961 with his retirement. In most cases his share was a flat 10 percent.

Although the lack of a formal education is apparent in his poor grammar, Eddie must have been very good in the arithmetic class. He is a multimillionaire from his track earnings and his shrewd business sense with investments. With the exception of stock market and oil speculation his money has been kept in and around racing, which he dearly loves. He has a share in a saddlery business which sells equipment to racing people all over the country, and spends most of his time at the Manhattan offices of his Livestock and Casualty Insurance Company, which provides coverage for every possible facet of the racing business. A top winner of stakes for 11 years, he is the author of *I Ride to Win*.

Arcaro lives in Garden City, Long Island, with his wife and two children, not far from another great jockey of yesteryear, Earl Sande, who resides in Munsey Park, Long Island. (Another legend of the racetrack, Ted Atkinson, is a State Steward at Arlington Park in Illinois.) When Eddie is not attending most of the major races around the country, he fits in some golf.

Now a businessman. *Millie Cole*

In 1926 she had youth, integrity, and the kind of pluck that America loves in its idols.

GERTRUDE EDERLE

The first woman to swim the English Channel was the daughter of a German emigrant who ran a delicatessen on Amsterdam Avenue in Manhattan. When Trudy, as she usually is called, first became interested in swimming her father told her that if she did well he would give her permission to bob her hair.

Miss Ederle was a product of the famed Women's Swimming Association, which has produced such champions as Eleanor Holm (an interior decorator now in Miami Beach, Florida) and Esther Williams (living in retirement in Los Angeles). She joined the club when she was thirteen years old—five years before conquering the Channel—and set about to break and establish more amateur records than any woman in the world.

Her first attempt at the Channel was financed by the W.S.A. in 1925. It was a valiant try, but she finally admitted defeat.

When she returned to Cap Gris Nez in France for her next attempt it was with a contract from both the New York *Daily News* and Chicago *Tribune,* paying her expenses, a modest salary, and bonus in exchange for exclusive rights to her personal story, plus the jump on every other newspaper in the country.

Among the party aboard the boat alongside Gertrude on August 6, 1926, were Westbrook Pegler and his wife, Julie Harpman, Westbrook "ghosting" the swimmer's account of her experience for the *Tribune.*

By the twelfth hour the sea had become so troubled by unfavorable winds that her trainer, Thomas Burgess, shouted to her, "Gertie, you must come out!" The exhausted girl lifted her head from the choppy waters and asked, "What for?"

Only five men had been able to swim it before. The best time had been 16 hours, 33 minutes by the Argentinian, Enrique Tiraboschi. Gertrude walked up the beach at Dover, England, after 14 hours and 31 minutes. The first person to greet her was an English immigration officer who asked the bleary-eyed, waterlogged teenager for her passport.

Instead of immediately returning to this country she visited her grandmother in Germany's Black Forest, for nearly three weeks. By the time she came back another woman, Mrs. Mille Gade Corson, had swum the Channel, although it took her an hour longer.

In addition to a few endorsements and an appearance in a Bebe Daniels movie, *Swim, Girl, Swim* (1927), Gertrude toured vaudeville in a swimming act for two years.

To understand why Miss Ederle was the idol she was at the time it is necessary to remember that the period was the Roaring Twenties. Everything was exaggerated. She was the first and the fastest, but she was also simple, unassuming, loyal, and very likable. Add to this the reports in the United States press that both England and France had been against her effort, hoping that one of their countrywomen might do it first, and you have the ingredients that turned New York City into a madhouse when Grover Whalen and Jimmy Walker escorted her during a ticker tape parade not to be equaled until Lindbergh came back in 1927.

Captain Patterson, publisher of the *Daily News,* gave her a red Buick Roadster as an added bonus. Most of the money she received was turned over to the Women's Swimming Association, which had given her the chance in the first place.

She was engaged once but has never married. After a nervous breakdown in the early thirties she suffered from an accident in 1933 which put her in a cast for over four years. In 1939 she made a comeback at the New York World's Fair when she appeared in Billy Rose's Aquacade.

In retrospect, Gertrude Ederle seems an even more exceptional personality than she was thought during the time of the parades and banquets. She had to give up the athlete's cherished amateur standing in order even to attempt what she did. Although with the proper management she could have been very rich, she has never uttered a word of bitterness about her financial circumstances. Her head was so buffeted about by the large waves that day in 1926 that her hearing was permanently impaired. Instead of asking for sympathy she has employed empathy by spending a great deal of time over the years teaching deaf youngsters to swim.

Trudy shuns publicity. She shares a house in Flushing, Queens, with an old friend.

Conducting one of her Saturday morning swimming classes at the Women's Swimming Association in Manhattan. *Wide World*

The Astaires appearing together on Broadway in *Apple Blossoms*, 1919.

ADELE ASTAIRE

The famous dancer was born Adele Austerlitz in 1899 in Omaha, Nebraska. Her father was a brewer, and her mother was determined to see that her daughter—and son Fred—would become stars in the theatre. At the age of three Adele was enrolled in a dancing school in Omaha, and when she was eight both brother and sister were brought by their mother to New York, where they studied with Ned Wayburn and at the Metropolitan Ballet School.

From 1906 until 1916 Fred and Adele toured the United States with the Orpheum and Keith vaudeville circuits. When not booked for an engagement they attended school in Weehawken, New Jersey.

The Astaires made their Broadway debut in the show *Over the Top* in 1917, and took it on tour. *The Passing Show of 1918* was their first big success, and they played in it both on Broadway and on the road. Their co-stars were Charles Ruggles, the late Frank Fay, and Nita Naldi. After that their names were on Broadway marquees every season.

John Charles Thomas the singer was with them in *Apple Blossoms* (1919), Adele playing Molly, and again in *Love Letter* (1921) when Adele played the role of Aline Moray.

In 1922 Fred and Adele sang and danced in two shows, *For Goodness Sake* and *Bunch and Judy*. The former became the vehicle for their London debut in 1923, although the title was changed in England to *Stop Flirting*. They became instant favorites in Britain.

In 1924 the team did George Gershwin's *Lady Be Good* with an assist from the late Cliff Edwards. It was an enormous hit in New York as well as in London, where they played in it in 1926.

In 1930 they were seen in *Smiles.* The next season, 1931, was to include the last musical the Astaires ever did together and the last Broadway ever saw of Adele. The show was *The Bandwagon,* and despite a Depression year it did well at the box office.

One of their most successful shows was another one which Gershwin wrote especially for them, *Funny Face* which they did on Broadway in 1927 and in London in 1928. Adele made up her mind that when she left show business it would be after a solid hit. She met Lord Charles Cavendish and promised to marry him, provided *The Bandwagon* was equally successful in London. (It was a smash, they were married in 1932.)

Unlike a lot of actresses, Adele meant it when she said good-bye to the boards. Composers, producers, and her brother begged her on various occasions to do just one more but she has never relented. When Fred tried working with another partner, Claire Luce (who is now teaching theatre in New York), one critic wrote that he seemed to sense him looking off into the wings, wondering when Adele would enter.

Each of Adele's three children by Lord Charles died shortly after birth. After her husband's death in 1944 she moved back to New York where she met and married a Wall Street investment broker, Kingman Douglass.

Mrs. Douglass divides her time among her homes in Middleburg, Virginia; on Manhattan's East 57th Street; and on the lush beaches of Jamaica. She is very social, very rich, and very uncommunicative to interviewers.

Accepting an award given to them by *Dance Magazine* recently. *Dance Magazine*

In 1934, at the height
of her fame.

RUBY KEELER

The musical star, born in Nova Scotia and moving to New York at age three with her family, went into show business as a dancer in speakeasies during the Roaring Twenties because it was the only profession that permitted high school girls to work nights. The money she received came in very handy at home where her mother had a houseful of children to care for.

She was in the chorus at Texas Guinan's El Fey Club when she caught the eye of a man who was at that time the biggest name on Broadway, Al Jolson. She became Mrs. Jolson in 1928. Jolson helped place Ruby in the Great Ziegfeld's *Show Girl* (1929). Every night she would do a tap dance onstage while Jolson strolled down the aisle of the theatre to a front row seat singing the song "Liza." Jolson received no billing and no money. It was the one and only time he ever worked for Flo Ziegfeld.

Jolson and Ruby were married in New York, and came to Hollywood in the early thirties when nearly all of the films being made were taking advantage of the new sound systems by adding songs.

Ruby was an unknown to movie audiences when Warner Brothers took a chance on her by giving her the lead in the 1933 film *42nd Street*. It was one of the most successful pictures that studio ever made and is today considered the classic musical of the 1930's. Her costar was a young man not much better known than Ruby, Dick Powell. Ruby and Dick costarred in a series of singing and dancing films such as *Dames* (1934), and *Shipmates Forever* (1935). Also in 1935 she and Al Jolson appeared together in a picture about backstage life called *Go Into Your Dance*.

76

Altogether Ruby Keeler made nine films, her last, *Sweetheart of the Campus* (1941), before she retired in 1941. She and Al Jolson had been divorced a year before she gave up movies, remaining in California, and was not heard from until *The Jolson Story* appeared. Ruby was awarded custody of their adopted son, Al, Jr.

When Columbia Pictures decided to make *The Jolson Story* (1947) they offered her a goodly sum of money for the use of her name. She refused to grant permission, and when the picture was made Mrs. Jolson, played by Evelyn Keyes, was given a fictitious name. (Evelyn is married to Artie Shaw.)

In 1966 when tributes to Busby Berkeley, her former director, were held in nine cities throughout South and North America and Europe, Ruby toured and appeared with her old friend. As the director's works were screened she stood in the back of one of the theatres and shook her head. "It's really amazing. I couldn't act. I had that terrible singing voice, and now I can see I wasn't the greatest tap dancer in the world, either."

All of what Miss Keeler said may be true, but she had a quality during those bleak Depression years that people could identify with. Her parts, those of a kid trying to get a break on Broadway, were so close to her own story that it didn't matter how she read the lines because she felt them, and the audiences were rooting for her to make good.

For more than twenty years Ruby Keeler has been the wife of John Lowe, a prominent Southern California land developer. They live with their four teenage children near the Pacific Ocean in Newport Beach, California. (Two of their neighbors are Cass Daley and Evelyn Ankers.) She is well known as one of the best lady golfers in those parts.

At a recent public appearance with her former director, Busby Berkeley. *Paul Cordes—Gallery of Modern Art*

In 1938, the year of his "grand slam."

DONALD BUDGE

Donald Budge at eighteen years of age won his native state's (California's) Junior Championship in 1933 and made the Davis Cup team two years later. By 1937 the boy whose older brother had to coax him away from football onto the tennis courts played 12 championship matches and won every one of them: his Davis Cup matches against Germany, Japan, Australia, and England (doubles with Gene Mako), plus the United States, Australian, and Wimbledon singles.

His 1937 game against Germany's champion, Baron von Cramm, is still talked about among tennis buffs as one of the most incredible exhibits of the game ever staged. The match was also the occasion for an international incident in the world of sports. The loser was imprisoned by Hitler's government upon his return on a morals charge which many thought was nothing more than punishment by the Nazi government. Had Von Cramm won that year the coveted Davis Cup would have gone to Germany for the first time in history. As a protest Budge refused an invitation to play in Germany the following year.

Of all Budge's many awards the one he prizes most is the James E. Sullivan Memorial Trophy for the Most Outstanding Amateur Athlete of 1937.

In 1938 he created a record that has never been equaled. He won the Australian, French, Wimbledon, and United States (Forest Hills) singles championships, which in the world of tennis is a "grand slam."

78

His partner for the mixed doubles at Wimbledon in the games of 1937 and 1938 was Alice Marble, now secretary to a doctor in Tarzana, California.

A story widely circulated and never denied concerns Budge during his first trip to Wimbledon. It is the custom of the Queen to arrive a bit late for the games. Queen Elizabeth, wife of George VI, was regally tardy, and Budge and his opponent had their game interrupted by her entrance. It is the custom for the players to wait until Her Majesty is seated, bowing toward the Royal box before resuming their game. Don, instead, lifted his racket in a salute and yelled, "Hi, Queen!"

Donald's first professional match was held in Madison Square Garden on January 3, 1939, and 16,000 fans filled the auditorium. Thereafter he toured the country for a number of years as the top draw in his field.

Through the years Donald has been involved in a number of business ventures. From 1941 until 1965 he was a partner with Sidney Wood in the Budge-Wood laundries in the Bronx. He now divides his year in thirds: in the summer he is in charge at the Chatham Hall School, one of the oldest and finest boys' schools in Virginia; in the fall and spring he commutes between the Racquet Club in Montego Bay, Jamaica, and the Peach Tree Bath and Tennis Club in Atlanta, Georgia. The remaining months he reserves for a vacation to be taken wherever he pleases.

Budge has remained active in his game, and his two books *On Tennis* and *How Lawn Tennis Is Played* are still basic for any serious participant.

In a recent visit to New York.
Bachrach

Fifteen-year-old Beverly, shortly after Errol Flynn's death in 1959.

BEVERLY AADLAND

Who could ever forget that real-life Lolita, Beverly Aadland.

She was a fifteen-year-old dancer when the late Errol Flynn met her. Together they made a dreadful movie called *Cuban Rebel Girl,* a lot of vulgar headlines, and according to Beverly, beautiful love. Her mother, the late Flo Aadland, told about it in the opening passage of her book *The Big Love:* "I want the world to know that my baby was a virgin when she met Errol Flynn."

For all the jokes about her at the time and since, Beverly must have had something. She was far from being a great beauty. In fact she is more attractive now than at the time of her fame. Yet Flynn, who never lacked for female companionship, and Beverly remained together until his death in 1959.

In 1960, after a series of unfortunate incidents in the Aadland household, Beverly, still a minor, was taken away from her mother by court order, and custody was given to the wife of a Pasadena, California, minister. At first Beverly did not take to the comparatively quiet atmosphere, but by the time she left the family at eighteen years of age they had become and still are close friends. In 1964, when she was nearly killed in an automobile wreck, her former guardian was the first to lend a helping hand. In 1965, when Mrs. Aadland died, it was the minister's wife that Beverly leaned on.

During the early sixties Beverly finally evaded the press which had dogged her every footstep. She left Southern California, where she was born and raised, and married and divorced a young architect with practically no fanfare.

80

In 1966 a New York daily reported Miss Aadland to be a stripper on the burlesque circuit. A simple phone call to her agent would have disclosed that Beverly was at that very moment playing a club date in the Midwest. She is and has been a singer in supper clubs for several years, playing such smart bistros as The Living Room in Manhattan.

Beverly has lost a lot of the defensiveness that she displayed at the height of her notoriety. She is quite courteous to interviewers, and answers questions about Flynn willingly. In reply to a query about the difference in their ages she replied recently, "At the time I was all over the front pages I really believed there was something very unusual about it. After he was gone and I got a good look at life up close I wonder what all the excitement was about. Younger girls and older men fall in love every day. Nobody says anything about it, and it certainly doesn't get into the papers—unless one of the two parties happens to be a movie star. One of these days somebody in a city room of a newspaper is going to get wind of a woman who happens to like a younger fellow, and two more people are going to be crucified."

Miss Aadland admits to several suicide attempts and periods of horrible depression when she was at the zenith of her fame, but seems to have come through it all with more than a usual amount of self-confidence for a girl in her early twenties.

Asked about her ambitions she says, "I think I'd like to own my own club. I like to entertain, and get along pretty well with the general public."

For over two years Beverly has been living in Springfield, Massachusetts. Why? She likes the town, and the newspapers are friendly. Before they print something they check it out with her for accuracy. But for an unmarried girl to settle in a comparatively small town seems unlikely. "What's swinging there? What do you do?" old friends ask her. "I learned to cook and I love it. Besides, at my house Springfield does swing," is Beverly's reply.

Now a chanteuse, she has blossomed into a beautiful woman.

In 1922 at a time when she was one of the reigning queens of the silent screen.

BLANCHE SWEET

Blanche Sweet was the name given, quite aptly, to a beautiful child born in 1895. "B. Sweet," as she signs her checks, was to become one of the earliest and greatest of silent stars.

Miss Sweet was a protégée of the great director D. W. Griffith, and was with him from 1909 on at the Biograph Studios on Manhattan's 14th Street. Until 1913 when she starred in the four-reeler *Judith of Bethulia* she appeared in shorter photoplays such as *Smile of a Child* (1911) and *Eternal Mother* (1912). Mae Marsh and the Gish sisters, always thought of as very early players in silents, had only small roles in *Judith of Bethulia* in support of Miss Sweet.

Her screen image was less delicate than those of most of her contemporaries. In a number of her early pictures such as *Goddess of Sagebrush Gulch, Fighting Blood,* and *The Last Drop of Water* she was the Pioneer Woman. When all the others had dropped by the wayside, Blanche was still whipping the oxen. Her most famous film of this type was *The Lonedale Operator* (1911).

In 1922 she married Marshall "Mickey" Neilan, director of such milestones as *Rebecca of Sunnybrook Farm* (1917) with Mary Pickford and *Tess of the D'Ubervilles* (1923), one of Miss Sweet's best remembered efforts. She and Neilan were divorced in 1929.

Her competition in *In the Palace of the King* (1923) was the original "It" girl, Aileen Pringle, now living in retirement in Manhattan. She costarred with Neil Hamilton (now playing the Chief of Police on TV's *Bat Man* series) in *Diplomacy* (1926). Ben Lyon was her leading man in *Bluebeard's Seven Wives* (1926).

Blanche Sweet made only three talkies, all in 1930. In *Woman Racket,* which Jean Harlow's husband Paul Bern directed, she not only spoke on the screen but sang as well. *Show Girl in Hollywood* gave her another chance to sing, but neither picture clicked with the fans. Her last appearance in movies was a minor role in Rex Beach's *The Silver Horde.*

After her failure in talkies Blanche became a vaudeville entertainer and achieved considerable success. She toured the United States in the early thirties with an act called *Sweet and Lovely.* For both the Fanchon Marco and Orpheum circuits she was a good draw with songs, comedy skits, and a scene from one of her most popular silents, *Anna Christie.*

Her last husband was Raymond Hackett, whom she met on the Metro-Goldwyn-Mayer lot several years before they were both offered parts in the road company of the play *The Party's Over* in 1935. She admits that the main reason she took the part was to get to know the handsome young man better. In 1936 they were married and lived together until he died in California in 1963. Throughout the thirties the husband and wife team did road shows of plays which had been hits on Broadway. Hackett, who had the advantage of stage experience, was of great help to cinema-oriented Blanche.

She and Hackett had been living quietly in retirement in Los Angeles for over twenty years. Upon his passing she moved back to the East where she was born and got her start in pictures.

Blanche Sweet lives in an apartment on Lexington Avenue within walking distance of where the famous Biograph Studios once stood. NBC Television recently did a documentary on those days, and Blanche appeared as the narrator. She would like to work a bit, but only if she really feels the part suits her. She has refused many offers for her autobiography, which she maintains she will never write.

In a recent television appearance.
NBC

Both in and out of character in 1941. "Lum" (Chester Lauck) on left and "Abner" (Norris Goff) on right.

LUM 'N' ABNER

In 1930 a bank clerk by the name of Chester Lauck quit his job and joined up with his lifelong friend, Norris Goff, who in turn left his job in the wholesale grocery business, to form a comedy team for a radio station in Hot Springs, Arkansas. Their original idea was to do a black-face act, but the director convinced them that since the success of "Amos 'n' Andy" there had been too many imitators. On April 26, 1931, the characters "Lum 'n' Abner" were born. In the twenty-three years that followed on radio there was not a single letter of complaint.

Their success at playing two small-town bachelor hicks was immediate. Within months they were signed by NBC. The show became so popular that it was broadcast over NBC's Red and Blue networks simultaneously. Their first sponsor was Quaker Oats, followed over the years by the Ford Motor Company, Horlick's Malted Milk, and Frigidaire.

"Lum" was played by Chester Lauck and "Abner" by Norris Goff, but they also played many of the other colorful bumpkin characters they used on the show. They made the mythical town of Pine Ridge, Arkansas, so famous that a little town in that state went to the trouble of getting an act of Congress to change its name to capitalize on the publicity.

Chester and Norris were born and raised in Mena, Arkansas, and knew their country people well. Rather than being annoyed by the ribbing given them by the pair, it was shown that the biggest audiences the shows had were in rural areas, where there are still "Jot 'em Down" general stores in many small towns. They got the name for their establishment after running a national contest in the thirties.

"Lum 'n' Abner" had more than a leisurely pace and folksy humor. In a 1948 review *Variety* said of the team who did their own scripts: "Some of the cracks would have done credit to the writing stables of higher-rated comics." Although the programs never had high ratings, the sponsors were kept happy with the sales results from the low-keyed and well-integrated commercials. The comics' mail averaged 15,000 letters a week and went as high as 23,000.

Some of the performers who were regulars on the series were Zasu Pitts, Andy Devine, and a character actor who wasn't as well known then by the name of Cliff Arquette, "Charlie Weaver."

In 1939 they began making movies, such as *Dreaming Out Loud* (1940), *Bashful Bachelors* (1942), and *Two Weeks to Live* (1943). As an example of their popularity, *Bashful Bachelors* cost $165,000 to produce and grossed $675,000 in one year on domestic release alone. Throughout their career in movies they had to wear heavy makeup which required two and a half hours of preparation each morning before they came on the set. Says Abner, "We have grown into our parts."

In 1954, just about the time that most of radio's big names were making the switch to television, Norris "Abner" Goff was told that he had to have an operation because of a cancer. Abner had wanted to retire anyway, and this was a perfect time to do so. Although the operation was a success, and he has been in good health since then, he has been reported dead by the press four times. He is visited several times a year by his friend and former partner at his home right on the green at the Indian Wells Golf Club in Palm Desert, California.

When Abner called it quits Lum decided to go into the oil business. He is the Executive Assistant to the Chairman of the Board of the Continental Oil Company in Houston, Texas, and is on the road a good deal of the time doing public relations work for the firm. His handshaking and after-dinner speaking have taken him over one and a half million miles since going into the business.

To queries about missing show business Lum says, "I feel like I'm still in it with the traveling and applause. And then, radio has changed so much there seems to be no place for shows like ours. Abner said when we went off the air that he was 'awful fer behind in my sittin',' and that's the business he's in right now—sittin' and lots of it. He never really enjoyed it the way I did, anyway, so I guess things worked out pretty well for both of us."

"Lum" Chester Lauck today.

LARRY PARKS

The Al Jolson impersonator, whose real name is Samuel Klausman, was born in Olathe, Kansas, in 1914. After receiving a B.S. from the University of Illinois he came to New York City where he ushered at Carnegie Hall and was a guide at Radio City.

Larry worked in stock companies in the mid-thirties and finally got a role in the 1937 Broadway production of *Golden Boy*. After several more years of stock and small parts he turned up in Hollywood in 1941.

Few actors worked more than Parks in the early forties, and it would be hard to find anyone who made worse films. A few of the clinkers Columbia Pictures put him in during that period are: *Mystery Ship* (1941) with Lola Lane (owner of a real estate business in Pacific Palisades, California), *Honolulu Lu* (1941), *You Belong to Me* (1941) a Barbara Stanwyck-Henry Fonda starrer, *Sing for Your Supper* (1941), *Blondie Goes to College* (1942) with Arthur Lake (married to the niece of Marion Davies and living in a huge home in Santa Monica, California), *Hello, Annapolis* (1942) which starred Tom Brown (who turns up from time to time on TV and lives in Sherman Oaks, California), *You Were Never Lovelier* (1942) a Rita Hayworth and Fred Astaire picture, *Boogie Man Will Get You* (1942), *Black Parachute* (1944), *Sergeant Mike* (1944), *Racket Man* (1944) with Tom Neal (serving a manslaughter sentence in a California prison for the death of his wife), and *Counter-Attack* (1945). In some years he made as many as a dozen pictures.

Then in 1946 something happened to Parks that usually happens only in the plot of a picture. Columbia gave him the role of Al Jolson in *The Jolson Story*. The songs were dubbed by Jolson himself, but the rest was all Larry Parks. He had survived a score of B pictures to become overnight one of the hottest leading men in the business. The Academy of Motion Pictures Arts and Sciences nominated him for the Best Actor of the Year. The film created box office records that still hold in some cities.

Columbia quickly put him into *Down to Earth* (1947) with Rita Hayworth and *The Swordsman* (1948). Metro-Goldwyn-Mayer wanted to borrow him for a picture with Elizabeth Taylor, but had to wait until he completed the sequel, *Jolson Sings Again* (1950).

In 1951 the House Un-American Activities Committee descended upon Hollywood. The very first witness called before that body was Larry Parks. Before he could even be asked the big question, the actor volunteered the information that he had been a member of the Communist party in the early forties and pointed out that he had left the party some years before. "The only loyalty I know is to America," he said in an emotional examination. After begging the Committee not to make him name names of fellow Hollywoodites the hearings were closed to the public. After his testimony in closed session a spokesman for H.U.A.C. said that Parks had "come through in fine style." The word around town was that he had given at least a dozen names of film personalities.

While the uproar over the affair continued, other stars, Lucille Ball, for one, paraded before the Committee and admitted party membership in the past. It was Parks, however, who made the headlines, and Columbia looked frantically for a loophole in his contract, which was canceled shortly thereafter. M-G-M released *Love Is Better Than Ever* (1951) which starred him with Elizabeth Taylor, but with little enthusiasm. John Wayne, one of filmdom's strongest supporters of H.U.A.C., asked that Hollywood forgive Larry his mistake and remember that he had been man enough to tell the truth.

Larry Parks was never blacklisted as were some 300 others, such as Alvah Bessie (recently living in San Francisco and working as a lighting director at a nightclub) or Karen Morley (residing in Los Angeles and still without work). He was more of an embarrassment to the industry—he couldn't be a *cause célèbre* because he had cooperated, and the right wing wasn't altogether happy with him, either.

Larry appeared on TV in plays in 1953, 1956, and 1958 and played on Broadway for a short time in 1957 with his wife in *The Bells Are Ringing*. Of the play, *Variety* said he was "more skillful as both singer and hoofer" than Sydney Chaplin, for whom he was substituting. He did two Broadway shows, one in 1960 and one in 1963, but both flopped. He was in John Huston's *Freud* (1962) in a prominent role, but the film was not a commercial success. His last engagement was a road tour of the play *Any Wednesday* in 1965.

Parks has been married to Betty Garrett, also of stage and films, since 1944. They live in the Nichols Canyon section of Hollywood with their two sons.

The Jolson Story, one of the hottest properties in movies, and in *Freud* (*right*), a rare appearance. *Universal Pictures*

A Universal Pictures contract player in 1937.

ELLA LOGAN

When she was three years old Ella Logan, the girl who introduced "How Are Things in Gloccamorra?" in the show *Finian's Rainbow,* walked onto the stage of the Grand Theatre in Paisley, Scotland, and made her debut singing "A Perfect Day." Ella (her real name is Ella Allan, born in 1913 in Scotland) stopped that show and has been stopping others ever since.

After a series of music hall tours in Great Britain, Ella came to London in 1928 in the show *Darling, I Love You,* and in 1931 and 1932 she appeared in vaudeville in Holland and Germany.

It was in 1934 that she made her Broadway debut, appearing in *Calling All Stars* with Judy Canova and Gertrude Niesen and two years later made her first motion picture, *Flying Hostess.* The following year she made *Woman Chases Man* with Miriam Hopkins and Joel McCrea, *Top of the Town* with the future California Senator George Murphy, and *52nd Street* with Kenny Baker, now retired in Solvang, a Danish community in California, and in 1938 was in the all-star *Goldwyn Follies.* One of her costars was the beautiful Vera Zorina who is married to the head of Columbia Records, Goddard Lieberson.

Ella returned to New York and musical comedy in the *George White Scandals of 1939,* the last of producer White's famous shows, and in its cast were Ben Blue and Ann Miller.

Throughout the late thirties and into the forties Miss Logan was a popular guest vocalist on some of the top radio shows of the day. In 1940 she was one of the featured performers in the summer replacement program for the *Eddie Cantor Show* on CBS. With her were Igor Gorin and Jacques Renard and his orchestra.

In 1941, she was with the late Carmen Miranda in the Olsen and Johnson show *Son o' Fun* and in 1942 in *Show Time* with Jack Haley, the De Marcos, George Jessel, and Kitty Carlisle.

In 1944, 1945, and 1946 Ella toured Africa, Italy, and other parts of Europe, entertaining Allied troops. When she returned to the United States in 1947 it was to play in what proved to be the highlight of her career, the part of Sharon McLonergan in the smash hit *Finian's Rainbow*. The show ran for over 500 performances, and introduced such standards as "Old Devil Moon," "Look to the Rainbow," "When I'm Not Near the Girl I Love," and, of course, the song that has been associated with Ella ever since, "How Are Things in Gloccamorra?" For reasons she has never adequately explained, Ella Logan has not been seen on Broadway since.

In 1956 Ella divorced Fred Finklehoff, writer and producer of plays— with a personal fortune of several million—after four years of marriage.

Since leaving Broadway Ella has appeared in the title role of a show called *Maggie* on the strawhat circuit, and at such nightclubs as the Monsignor, Piccadilly, and Ambassadors in London as well as Ciro's and Scheherezade in Paris. She has also done an occasional television show for Ed Sullivan and Jack Paar.

Recently Miss Logan accepted a part in the musical *Kelly*, produced by David Susskind. The show received a great deal of fanfare, costing its backers just short of $750,000. The day after it opened in New York the critic for *The New York Times* began his review by congratulating Ella Logan for having the good sense to step out of this production before it reached Broadway. It closed after one performance.

Ella Logan maintains a house in Mandeville Canyon in Los Angeles and an apartment in New York City.

In a New York restaurant recently.
John Virzi

In 1925.

CHESTER CONKLIN

One of the silent screen's all-time great funnymen, Chester was born in Oskaloosa, Iowa, on January 11, 1886. Before becoming a clown with the Barnum Circus he traveled the country for a while as part of a stock company.

Chester found his way into pictures in 1913 and appeared in most of the Chaplin one-reelers made in 1914. Two classics from that period are: *Face on the Bar Room Floor* and *Between Showers*.

In 1915 he became a Keystone Cop, with such beauties as Gloria Swanson, Mable Normand, and Marie Prevost as foils for his nonsense, and continued working for Mack Sennett for four years.

Although he worked steadily through the twenties and into the thirties, Conklin's days of glory ended when he left Sennett, though he did appear in such silents as *Greed* (1923) the Erich von Stroheim masterpiece, *A Woman of the World* (1925) with Pola Negri, *Sybil* (1926) with Constance Talmadge, and *Rubber Heels* (1927) with Ed Wynn.

Conklin, who made as much as $3,500 a week at the peak of his career, lost everything in the stock market crash of 1929. In 1933 Chester and Minnie V. Conklin, his wife of 19 years, were divorced.

His sound films include: *The Virginian* (1929), *Swing High* (1930) with Helen Twelvetrees (who committed suicide in 1958), *Her Majesty Love* (1931) with Marilyn Miller and W. C. Fields, *Call of the Prairie* (1936) with William Boyd, *Hollywood Boulevard* (1936) in which he played himself, *Modern Times* (1936) with his old friend Charlie Chaplin, *Every Day's a Holiday* (1938) which starred Mae West, *Cinema Circus* (1939) a two-reeler for MGM with Lee Tracy, *Hollywood Cavalcade* (1939) with Don Ameche

90

(now a resident of Phoenix, Arizona), *The Great Dictator* (1940) another Charlie Chaplin feature, *Hail the Conquering Hero* (1944) with Ella Raines (now Mrs. Robin Olds of Washington, D.C.), *Goodnight, Sweetheart* (1944) with Ruth Terry (now Mrs. Gilmour of North Hollywood, California), *Sunday Dinner for a Soldier* (1944) with the late John Hodiak, *Knickerbocker Holiday* (1944) with Nelson Eddy, *The Perils of Pauline* (1947), *The Beautiful Blonde from Bashful Bend* (1949), and *Jiggs and Maggie in Jackpot Jitters* (1949).

In 1954 newspapers throughout the country carried a sad feature article datelined Los Angeles. Chester Conklin, who had found acting jobs in movies hard to come by, was playing Santa Claus at J. W. Robinson's Department Store. The aging comic took the notoriety very well and told the reporters that he liked acting and kids, and that with this job he had lots of both. He did, however, appear in *Li'l Abner* in 1960.

In 1961 Chester checked into the Motion Picture Country Hospital with every intention of staying for the remainder of his life. He was not feeling well and was a little depressed over his lack of activity during the past years. The Hollywood community was advised accordingly by the trade press, confirming that one of the truly great comedians of their industry had retired.

Then in 1965 filmdom learned that the seventy-nine-year-old veteran was marrying June Gunther, whom he met in the hospital, and that the newlyweds would be moving to their own home in Van Nuys, California.

The Conklins live in a cottage complete with rose garden, which Chester tends faithfully. He says that he feels fine again and to prove it turned up in a small role recently in the Henry Fonda-Joanne Woodward starrer *A Big Hand for the Little Lady*.

A recent shot—not much change over nearly a half century.

Beside *Lizzy* in 1938.

DOUGLAS "WRONG WAY" CORRIGAN

The Atlantic Ocean had been crossed many times between Lindbergh's flight in 1927 and Corrigan's in 1938. All kinds of men in all kinds of planes had made the trip, but never—before or since—"by mistake."

Corrigan was a thirty-one-year-old mechanic who had been working at the Northrop Corporation aircraft works in Inglewood, California. Six years before he had bought a 1929 Curtis-Robin monoplane at an auction for $900. In 1937 he applied for permission to make a solo flight across the Atlantic, but after inspecting his plane the Bureau of Air Commerce had turned him down, advising him that they disapproved of suicide. The ship had no safety devices, no radio, and no beam finders. He had loaded it with so many extra gas tanks to carry the 320 gallons of gas and 16 gallons of oil, that he had to look out the side windows in order to see in front of him.

In mid-July, 1938, Douglas Corrigan flew from Los Angeles to Floyd Bennett Field in New York in 27 hours, but the feat went unnoticed in the wake of Howard Hughes's three-day trip around the world, which climaxed at the same time.

At dawn the next morning Corrigan advised the field's manager, Kenneth Behr, that he was going to fly back home. The ship was so heavy with fuel that it went 3,200 feet on the runway before taking off.

After 23 hours and 13 minutes he put "Lizzy," as he called the plane, down at Baldonnel Airport in Dublin. The date was July 17, 1938. "I've just flown from New York," said Corrigan to the startled airport officials. "My God, not in that thing!" someone cried. Then when he was told where he was, the pilot uttered the words that were to make him overnight a household word around the world: "I flew the wrong way."

92

Corrigan claimed his compass had got stuck and that he really had meant to fly to California. The story was so ridiculous and his delivery so barefaced it endeared him to his generation. He was like a throwback to the past decade, when foolishness was expected. But this was 1938, a grim Depression year. The more he told his story the more incredible it became. Altogether he had spent $100.15—$100 for gas, 10¢ for chocolate bars, and a 5¢ deposit on the bottle he took along, filled with drinking water. In London the United States Ambassador, Joseph P. Kennedy, congratulated him, America welcomed him home with a ticker tape parade down Fifth Avenue, and the press gave him the nickname "Wrong Way."

Corrigan made over $85,000 from endorsements and barnstorming appearances, and the 1939 movie based on his adventure, *The Flying Irishman* (in which he played himself). Thereafter he worked as a commercial pilot, and during World War II was in the Ferry Command, the civilian arm of the military flying aircraft for delivery abroad.

In 1946 he made an unsuccessful bid for the California Senate seat. After that he settled down with his wife and three sons in an orange grove in Santa Ana, California. His wife, Elizabeth, died in 1966.

In spite of his brazen act, Corrigan was always rather shy. Although he has lived in Santa Ana for about twenty years, the local paper has yet to be granted an interview with its only local celebrity. Letters requesting photographs and autographs go unanswered, and his neighbors agree that he keeps pretty much to himself.

In the middle of the orchard is an old barn, where he keeps "Lizzy." He hasn't decided whether to donate it to a museum or leave it to his children. The famous leather jacket he wore on the flight also is still in his possession.

Only recently someone asked him point blank if he really meant to fly back to Los Angeles, and he answered, "Sure. Well, at least I've told that story so many times that I believe it myself now."

Making certain the pilot is headed in the right direction during a recent flight to New York City. *Trans World Airlines*

HUBERT F. JULIAN: The "Black Eagle"

The world's most famous Negro aviator and soldier of fortune was born to a prosperous Trinidad plantation owner in 1897. His parents sent him to school in England, but when World War I broke out in Europe he was removed to Canada where he stayed until entering the United States in 1918.

Hubert Fauntleroy Julian came to the United States in order to patent his invention, a contraption bearing a crude resemblance to both a helicopter and a parachute. Although he was granted a patent, the machine never was put to practical use. He maintains that it is the basis for a device used to bring astronauts to earth after orbiting, and that it also inspired the helicopter.

While trying to promote his invention, and himself, he learned to fly an airplane. In 1922 during the Long Island Air Show, Julian became the first Negro to parachute from a plane over New York City. He readily admits that his chief motivation for attempting this seemingly senseless and dangerous stunt was to make himself known. Two years later, when even a transcontinental flight was a major feat, he announced his intention to fly from New York to Africa. His plane crashed into Flushing Bay, but Julian accomplished his objective—his daring, ridiculous flight had made him world famous. The press dubbed him the "Black Eagle of Harlem."

Through the rest of the 1920's, Julian lived in Harlem and continued to earn money and notoriety by stunt flying. In Harlem, he became friends with the black nationalist Marcus Garvey.

In 1930 he flew in an air show as part of the entertainment to celebrate the coronation of the new Emperor of Ethiopia, Haile Selassie. Julian's plane crashed. In 1932 he became a $100-a-day personal pilot to the religious leader, Father Divine, during that prophet's American barnstorming tour of what he called his "heavens."

Julian is probably best known for his Ethiopian Period—sometime after his introduction at the coronation air show, Emperor Haile Selassie gave him the rank of Colonel, and made him Military Governor of Ethiopia during the 1939 invasion by Mussolini.

In 1940 he came to his earlier employer's aid. During a trial in which Father Divine was being sued by one of his "angels" for the return of her $6,500, Colonel Julian marched into the courtroom and dramatically announced that he would personally settle the claim. When others came forth with similar demands, he withdrew the offer.

When in 1940 the Russians attacked Finland, Julian flew a fighter plane and with the rank of Captain led a squadron in the Finnish Air Force. During the Battle of Britain he challenged Field Marshal Hermann Goering to an air duel with Messerschmitts over the English Channel. The Germans replied to Julian's invitation to their Luftwaffe head by suggesting that the

Negro paint a black baboon on the side of his plane so that he could be readily identified.

During World War II he served for a short time in the Army Air Corps, thus becoming a citizen, but because he was considered too old for combat the Pentagon released him for the duration for a job with the Ford Motor Company's Willow Run aircraft plant near Detroit. After the war he served for a time as the head of Ethiopian Airlines.

During the 1948 elections Julian worked hard in Negro districts for Harry Truman, and was later sent to Germany to investigate reports of discontent among Negro troops during the Berlin airlift by the President's military aide, Major General Harry Vaughan.

In 1951 he and his wife purchased a duplex in the Bronx only a few minutes from Yankee Stadium, and Julian took out a license as a registered arms dealer, taking time out to dabble in gold purchases for foreign countries as well. In 1962 he was arrested and held for four months in Elisabethville, Katanga, charged by United Nations forces in the Congo with attempting to smuggle arms to his old friend, Moise Tshombe.

During the Watts riots of 1965 the Black Eagle arrived in London to announce that he was so ashamed of the behavior of some Negroes in the United States that he and his family were moving to England. He claims that it was only through the persuasion of "very important people in Washington" that he decided against giving up residence in the United States. On the subject of civil rights and the call for "Black Power" Julian says, "I am interested in Black Power, but through black productivity—not violence or defiance of authority."

Although he claims that he has grown too old for the high adventure he used to thrive on, the Colonel has lost none of his flamboyance. When he is not on a business trip to Bombay or Port-au-Prince he can be seen driving around the Bronx in a gold-fitted Rolls Royce, wearing custom-made English clothes, and with a monocle dangling from a black silk ribbon.

In 1934, making money and headlines flying for Ethiopia, and (*right*) disembarking at London on one of his frequent transatlantic business trips. *UPI*

MAGDA LUPESCU

Here was a story that asked the question: Can a little Jewish girl from the simple town of Hertza, Bessarabia, grow up to become the mistress to the King of Rumania, the most powerful woman in Eastern Europe, and a Princess? The answer is a resounding Yes.

Elena Wolff was born in 1896. Her father Latinized the family name shortly afterward to Lupescu. The press arbitrarily dubbed her "Magda" after her affair with Crown Prince Carol became known. At court in Bucharest she was referred to contemptuously as "the Lupescu." To her lover and friends she was always "Duduia." Elena has been called a few other names along the way, but none a lady would ever answer to.

For a brief time during World War I she was the wife of an artillery officer by the name of Tampaneau. They were divorced shortly after the Armistice. Exactly when and how she and Carol met is not certain. Most sources think it was in 1923. All agree that neither Carol nor his country was ever the same again after he came under her influence. He had a morganatic marriage to Zizi Lambrino, the daughter of a Rumanian general. After producing a son, Mircea (married to an American heiress and living in England), the marriage was annulled by his father, King Ferdinand, and Carol was wed to Princess Helen of Greece. Two years later, because of his relationship with Lupescu, he was exiled and his four-year-old son Michael assumed the throne upon the death of Ferdinand. Carol and Lupescu went off to live on the Riviera. Helen divorced him in 1928.

Carol returned to Rumania and the throne in 1930 without the Lupescu. She was, however, not far behind, and with her arrival the country's most colorful decade began. (Because of the "she-wolf," another one of her titles, Carol was never actually crowned.) During a family squabble Dowager Queen Marie was shot in the side, but those who knew Lupescu couldn't believe that she was that poor a shot.

One of the most powerful forces in Rumania was the fascist organization known as the Iron Guard. At the top of its list of those it considered enemies of the state was the Lupescu. That the King had a mistress was immoral. That this woman all but ruled Rumania was disagreeable. But that she was Jewish was too much. There were numerous plots and counterplots. A Prime Minister was assassinated, and for fear that he would be next Carol did not attend the funeral. Lupescu persuaded the King to ally with France rather than Germany, which made her even more unpopular. In 1938 Carol proclaimed himself Dictator, but no one paid much attention. By 1940 things had become so dangerous for them as the war spread in Europe, that he abdicated.

For nearly a decade they moved about from Spain to Mexico, from Cuba to Brazil, until the Lupescu in 1949 became "gravely ill." It was her last wish that she die as an honest woman and, incidentally, a princess. The ceremony brought miraculous results. In no time she was up and about giving everyone orders, as usual. Cynics said that she had nothing more than a minor fever, but if so it would have been the only minor thing she ever had in her life.

After Carol died in Portugal in 1952, to the amazement of most royalists, she was received by the German branch of the Royal House of Hohenzollern, thus making her title of Princess official. It was suggested at the time that the Hohenzollerns had in mind the many, many millions that Carol had taken with him when he left Rumania. It must have been a great disappointment to them to learn that Lupescu had a reputation for many things, but generosity was not among them.

Queen Helen lives in regal splendor in Italy. Her only son, Michael, who didn't get a single leu from his father, lives in Switzerland where he is engaged in international banking. Zizi Lambrino is dead.

Since Carol's death, the Lupescu has lived in seclusion in a palatial villa called Mar y Sol in Estoril, Portugal. She leaves her house, which overlooks the Mediterranean, from time to time for short trips to Paris and Switzerland. Exiled Rumanians in New York and Paris hear nothing from her, and very little of her. She used to keep a monkey and a parrot, but both are rumored as deceased. The only visitor she has that the international colony in Estoril knows of is her cousin who is married to a Portuguese Marquis. To while away the hours she plays cards, for companionship she has the former Marshal of the Royal Palace, a man called Urdareanu, and for comfort there is all that lovely money.

King Carol II and Lupescu in Paris, 1929. *Kermit Kelly*

Princess Elena now, accompanied by Prince Andrew of Yugoslavia, on a visit to the tomb of King Carol. *Wide World*

With Robert Woolsey (*left*) in a scene from their 1936 movie *Silly Billies*.

BERT WHEELER

As long ago as 1914 Bert Wheeler was a comedy headliner. At that time he was with his first wife, Betty, in vaudeville. They made as much as $1,500 a week, which was top money in those days when every bill in every theatre had at least one comedy act on it.

The Great Ziegfeld made no secret of his lack of interest in and appreciation for comedy. Since his shows always had a strong element of it, he was forced to hire the funny men and women by reputation alone. That Bert Wheeler worked for the producer twice is his proudest boast: "You could never get the stage to rehearse. He'd be using it to drape those gorgeous dames. You could rehearse in the alley for all he cared. But when you worked for Mr. Ziegfeld you had made it. That was the tops."

Wheeler's first show for Ziegfeld was the *Follies of 1923*. During the New York engagement Fanny Brice also starred in it, but she had another commitment and did not take it on the road. Before the show left she asked her good friend Wheeler to visit her husband, Nick Arnstein, who was doing time in Leavenworth Prison, when the show got to Kansas. When he went to the penitentiary Bert took with him the former Heavyweight Champion of the World, James J. Corbett, who was in the Follies that year doing a song and dance. When word got out that the great fighter was in the prison an actual riot ensued among the prisoners who wanted to see him. Wheeler and Corbett had to be taken from the grounds under heavy guard while the convicts were kept at bay with fire hoses.

In the 1920's Wheeler was one of the biggest names in show business. He worked at all of the top vaudeville houses in the country, and was countless times the name on the top of the bill at the Palace in New York.

To movie fans, Bert Wheeler is always a name associated with another— the team of Wheeler and Woolsey made over 30 movies during the thirties. They worked together for the first time in Ziegfeld's smash musical, *Rio Rita,* in 1927. The two comedians were the only members of the original cast taken to Hollywood for the motion picture version. The show that has become a standard for light opera companies over the years had its premiere in the Ziegfeld Theatre, which the producer had recently purchased and named for himself. It ran for over two and one-half years and boasted, along with other big names of the day, the Paul Whiteman Orchestra. (Whiteman lives with his wife, the former film star Margaret Livingston, in New Hope, Pennsylvania.)

Wheeler and Woolsey were the first comedy team to emerge as stars from sound films. All through the thirties they continued to turn out money-making comedies for RKO. Two of their best remembered were *Girl Crazy* (1932), the original movie version which Judy Garland and Mickey Rooney remade years later, and *So This Is Africa* (1933) a typical Wheeler and Woolsey piece of wackiness. One of the talents that was unleashed in several of their features was the amazing child comedienne, Mitzi Green, who is today married to movie director Joe Pevney.

Wheeler made a couple of movies after his partner died in 1938, but he was no longer comfortable in Hollywood without Woolsey. One was a colossal flop called *Las Vegas Nights* (1941) with Tommy Dorsey and his orchestra. Wheeler sang a song in it called "Dolores" while Dorsey's vocalist sat by. That singer was a young man from Hoboken, New Jersey, named Frank Sinatra.

The two trademarks of Wheeler and Woolsey pictures were Robert Woolsey's ever-present cigar and a cute little blonde by the name of Dorothy Lee, who after an unsuccessful marriage to Hollywood gossip columnist Jimmie Fidler, settled down in Chicago.

One of the best remembered stars of yesterday and best loved men in show business, Bert Wheeler is an honorary lifetime member of both the Friars and the Lambs clubs. Two of his fellow Lambs with whom Bert often spends an afternoon playing cards are the former actor-director-playwright Elliott Nugent and the character actor from stage and screen Bernard Nedell. He lives at the Lambs in New York City. Over the years he has done an occasional stint in summer stock, nightclub engagement, or guest shot on radio and television shows. Far from being retired he admits he is a bigger ham today than when he started. He has a new partner in Tommy Dillon, a young man who has worked with the veteran in Las Vegas and Manhattan's Latin Quarter in recent years.

Bert is an even bigger ham today.

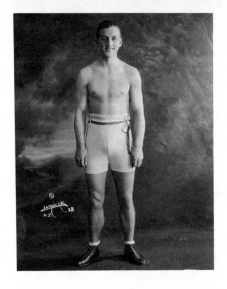

July 29, 1920,
Heavyweight Champion of Europe.

GEORGES CARPENTIER

Anyone meeting Georges Carpentier before the First World War would have guessed that he would be a success in whatever field he chose. He had looks, bearing, intelligence, and charm. He would certainly go far in the arts. He did, indeed, but the art was boxing. Georges mastered it, and in 1913 at the age of nineteen became the Heavyweight Champion of Europe by knocking out British fighter Bombardier Billy Wells in the first round.

Fame did not change Carpentier's style. In the ring it was the French pugilistic style called *savate*. Out of the ring it was sufficiently suave for him to knock about Paris with Colette, Chevalier, the Aga Khan, and Mistinguett.

Georges fought well in the war also and was awarded the *croix de guerre* and the *médaille militaire*. When it was over he retained his title by knocking out another Englishman, Joe Beckett, in only 74 seconds. One of the first to shake his hand afterward was the Prince of Wales, now the Duke of Windsor. The year was 1919.

The Dempsey-Carpentier bout was held on July 1, 1921, at Boyles' Thirty Acres in Jersey City, New Jersey. The match was promoted by the late Tex Rickard, who promised to pay both fighters a half million dollars each. The fees were considered so enormous that Rickard's backers withdrew. The promoter combined a genuine love of sports with an unfailing sense of the theatrical. He reasoned that Jack Dempsey would be a huge draw because he was very unpopular with the public and press at that time. The fighter had beaten charges of draft evasion in court, and he was not a sympathetic figure in the eyes of most people. (It is Rickard who is credited with making boxing a sport attended by women as well as men. Until then it was strictly a man's game.) Carpentier was cast as the good guy. He looked nothing like a prizefighter—he was handsome, and French to boot. The ladies would love him.

The match was called "The Fight of the Century." Americans were already familiar with Dempsey, and Ring Lardner introduced them to Carpentier: "He registers the most frightening agony in the ring. The only thing I have seen to match this phase of his art was John Barrymore's reaction to amputation as Captain Ahab in *Moby Dick*."

Frenchmen held high hopes for their Georges to return to France with the title. Planes were to fly over Paris dropping red flares if he won and white if he lost. H. L. Mencken gave an objective account of what happened: "Carpentier decayed like an autumn leaf in Vallambrosia. Gently and pathetically he fluttered down." It was a KO by Dempsey in the fourth round. But even defeat did not seem to mar his image. Lloyd George when he received the news spoke for France as well as England when he cabled Carpentier, "I admire you more than ever."

Rickard's gamble paid off. The gate was $1,789,238, the third largest in the history of boxing.

Carpentier held the World's Light Heavyweight Championship from 1920 until 1922, when he lost it to the Senegalese "Battling Siki," and gave up boxing completely after Gene Tunney defeated him in 1924 by a KO in the first round.

One of his most ardent fans was George Bernard Shaw who called him "the greatest boxer in the world."

During the late twenties and into the thirties Carpentier was an attraction on the music-hall stages of England and the Continent and in films. In 1930 he appeared in the early talkie-musical for Warner Brothers *Show of Shows*. Also in the cast were silent stars Viola Dana (now married to a golf pro and living in Santa Monica) and her sister Shirley Mason (living in West Los Angeles).

In 1935 Georges, who never felt comfortable as a performer, became a Parisian restaurateur. He is the proprietor of the restaurant in the Hôtel de Paris on the Right Bank, which has become a mecca for tourists looking for the finest in French cuisine and a glimpse of one of the Golden People of Sports.

Jack Dempsey takes a right from Carpentier while Tommy Loughran, Light Heavyweight Champion 1927–29, referees. The occasion was a recent showing of George Bellows fight drawings and paintings at the Gallery of Modern Art in New York City—*Paul Cordes— Gallery of Modern Art*

Under contract to
Twentieth Century-Fox, 1940.

ANNABELLA

The blonde film beauty of the thirties was born Suzanne Georgette Carpentier in 1910. She dropped all three of her names in favor of one, after reading Edgar Allan Poe's "Annabel Lee."

Annabella began working in motion pictures in 1930 when the distinguished director René Clair chose her for his film *Le Million* because, he said, she bore a striking resemblance to the silent star Bessie Love. Another of her pictures made in her native France was *Un Soir de Rafle* (1931).

In 1934 she was brought to Hollywood to costar in *Caravan* with Charles Boyer and Loretta Young, but her debut in American films was something less than sensational. She returned to Europe where she made movies in Hungary, Germany, and Austria, and by the late thirties Annabella was one of the most sought-after leading ladies in continental film making. By the time she caught the attention of United States moguls again her career was firmly established abroad.

The picture that brought Annabella to Hollywood in a blaze of publicity and enthusiasm was the first color film ever made in England, *The Wings of the Morning* (1937) which costarred Henry Fonda. Also featured was the Irish tenor John McCormack. The color process was glorious and Annabella was very appealing as the girl who masqueraded throughout much of the film as a boy. She was put under contract to Twentieth Century-Fox.

Some of her American films are: *Under the Red Robe* (1937) with Conrad Veidt, *Dinner at the Ritz* (1937) opposite Paul Lukas, *The Baroness and the Butler* (1938) which costarred William Powell, *Suez* (1938), in which she played opposite Tyrone Power. Her bathing scene in that picture was very daring for the time, and the studio made much of it in their publicity for the big-budget picture. What developed between Annabella and Power, however, proved to be much better box office than planned. When the actor was sent to Rio de Janiero on a public appearance tour his costar followed.

After a whirlwind courtship they were married in 1939 in the garden of Charles Boyer's home. Don Ameche was the best man, and Mrs. Boyer the maid of honor. During that year Annabella appeared in *Bridal Suite* with Robert Young.

In 1941 the couple appeared together on the strawhat circuit in *Liliom*. Power adopted her daughter by a previous marriage; she is now married to actor Oskar Werner.

The following year Annabella headed the Chicago company of Noel Coward's hit play *Blithe Spirit,* and in 1944 played on Broadway in *Jacobowsky and the Colonel.*

Brooks Atkinson in 1946 wrote in *The New York Times* of her performance in *No Exit:* "As the homosexual, Annabella is giving a bold and calculated performance that packs one corner of Hell with horror." The Jean-Paul Sartre play was directed by John Huston, and costarred Claude Dauphin. Thereafter she made *13 Rue Madeleine* (1947) with James Cagney.

Annabella had been given the complete Hollywood treatment. She endorsed Schaefer beer and attributed her complexion to Lux toilet soap, but unlike so many of the exotic beauties the film capital imported, the French star emerged with her distinct personality intact. Although none of her pictures were of exceptional quality, the lady was and could never be confused with any other actress in appearance or manner.

The Powers were divorced in 1948 with Annabella reportedly receiving a cash settlement, plus a yearly alimony of $70,000. The actor, who was her fourth and last husband, died of a heart attack in 1958.

In a recent interview Annabella lamented that she was forced to give up the American citizenship she took out in 1942 when she returned to France a number of years ago to take care of her aging mother. Although she still visits this country and says that in her heart she will always be an American, most of her time is spent on her farm, where she pastures a flock of sheep on her 26 acres, in the Pyrenees Mountains of France—not far from the château of silent star Eleanor Boardman.

Presenting the Best Actor Award to Gregory Peck for his performance in *To Kill a Mockingbird* during one of her visits. *Academy of Motion Picture Arts and Sciences*

In 1939.

PATSY KELLY

Patsy Kelly never received star billing or had her picture on the cover of *Photoplay,* but she has more fans than many of the big stars of her era.

The comedienne began her career on Broadway where she appeared in 1931 in *The Wonder Bar* opposite Al Jolson.

Hollywood cast her in a series of memorable comedies paired with Thelma Todd, the blonde counterpart to Miss Kelly. These two-reelers made for Metro-Goldwyn-Mayer are considered by authorities on screen comedy as among the finest the sound era produced. (They have not yet been released to television.) In 1935 Thelma Todd died of carbon monoxide poisoning under most peculiar circumstances. The case has never been solved.

The studio then put Patsy with Lyda Roberti in a series of comedy shorts, but that association was also ended when Lyda died in 1938.

In 1934 Patsy played Jean Harlow's best friend in *The Girl From Missouri.* The next year she made three of her best features: *Every Night at Eight* starring Alice Faye and Frances Langford (who divides her time between Florida and Chicago as the wife of the boat manufacturer, Ralph Evinrude), which was the film that introduced the song "I'm in the Mood for Love"; *Thanks a Million* in which she supported Dick Powell and Ann Dvorak (now living in Honolulu, Hawaii, with her husband, Nicholas Wade, the president of a chemical firm); and *Page Miss Glory,* appearing with Marion Davies.

Some of Miss Kelly's other credits are: *Sing, Baby, Sing* (1937), which was a spoof of the Elaine Barrie-John Barrymore antics; *Wake Up and Live* in which Patsy played the girl Friday of the star, Walter Winchell; and

Road Show in 1941 with the beautiful Carole Landis who committed suicide seven years later. The same year she had a supporting role in the RKO film *Playmates* in which John Barrymore received second billing to the popular orchestra leader of the day, Kay Kyser (he's still married to singer Georgia Carroll and lives in a small town in North Carolina where he is a practitioner of Christian Science). Another in the cast was Ish Kabibble (until recently a salesman for Ginny Simms's real estate development corporation. In 1966 he moved to Seattle, Washington, and another real estate job under his real name of Merwyn A. Bogue). In 1942 she appeared in *Sing Your Worries Away* with Bert Lahr.

None of her pictures could really be considered important, but in each Patsy's performance stands out as the highlight of the picture. Many times when some of her movies are shown on television after some thirty years, TV magazines and newspapers will recommend an otherwise dated film with the comment: "worth watching for the Patsy Kelly scenes." Her only peer was the late Joan Davis.

For reasons which have never really been made clear Patsy Kelly faded from pictures thereafter. In 1955 she toured the country with her old friend Tallulah Bankhead in a farce called *Dear Charles.* Patsy was onstage no more than 15 minutes, but at the final curtain she got as much applause as the star. It was more than just sentimentality on the part of the audience. Patsy took the small part and went wild with it. She was still a very funny lady.

Miss Kelly lives in Hollywood. She has never married. In 1960 she had a part in *The Crowded Sky,* and in 1966 she distinguished *The Ghost in the Invisible Bikini* by her appearance in it.

Today, still clowning. *American-International Pictures*

JAMES J. BRADDOCK

"The Cinderella Man," as he was called when he became World's Heavy-weight Champion, was born in New York's Hell's Kitchen in 1905. At sixteen he left his job as a printer's devil in favor of fighting for prizes and working as a sparring partner in local gyms for the professionals.

During 1926, his first year as a professional, Jim was undefeated in 16 fights, 11 of them won by knockouts. He beat some of the best boys around at the time: Phil Weisberger and Carmine Caggiano, both flattened, and Lew Barba, beaten on points; and in 1927 he took eight decisions and knocked out three men, Stanley Simmons, George La Rocca, and Johnny Alberts.

The next year he was matched with Pete Latzo, the ex-World Welter-weight Champion, in Newark. Against the odds Braddock not only whipped Latzo, who had been on his way to a comeback until that night, but broke his jaw along the way. Again that year, Braddock scored an upset when he defeated Tuffy Griffith in Madison Square Garden.

After losing a decision to Leo Lomski and KOing Jimmy Slattery, Jim was put up against one of the shrewdest and hardest hitting fighters in ring history, Tommy Loughran (see recent photo in Carpentier segment). In the Yankee Stadium on July 18, 1929, Braddock was made to look like a kid with his first pair of gloves. After that bitter lesson, Braddock lost to Yale Okun, Leo Lomski, Maxey Rosenbloom, and John Henry Lewis, among others, although during the same period, 1930–32, he knocked out Jake Warren and Phil Mercurio, and won a decision against Dynamite Jackson. It was far from being the record of an impending champion.

In 1933 he was losing as many as he was winning until on September 25 he cracked both hands in a bout with Abe Feldman. He couldn't fight, it was the middle of the Depression, and by this time he had a wife and three children to support. He was forced to work on the docks again in Hoboken, but even that wasn't steady enough to keep the Braddocks in food and clothing. In desperation James J. Braddock entered his name on the New Jersey relief rolls.

In 1934 the promoters of the Primo Carnera-Max Baer match were looking around for someone to fight the promising Corn Griffin in the semifinal bout preceding the main event. Although Braddock was considered retired, someone thought that the money he'd get for the beating he was sure to take would be of interest to him. It was. On June 14, 1934, the crowd that had come to see Baer and Carnera battle it out first watched Braddock hit the canvas in the first round, only to come back in the second frame with a right that KO'd Griffin to the amazement of all in the Long Island Bowl that night.

Again Braddock was supposed to be a scapegoat when he was set to fight John Henry Lewis on November 16, 1934. The opponent was younger, faster, and had the psychological advantage of having beaten Jim once before. But after ten blistering rounds, during which Braddock looked better than ever, he was given the decision.

He next met Art Lasky on March 22, 1935. Lasky was taller, had a greater reach, was 15 pounds heavier, and was favored by the experts and gamblers to win. From the first round straight through to the fifteenth Jim confounded all present by outsmarting and outpunching Lasky all the way.

The two leading contenders to fight Champion Max Baer were Max Schmeling and Jim Braddock. It was proposed that Schmeling fight Jim first, but Schmeling refused, thereby giving Braddock a crack at the title.

The twenty-nine-year-old Braddock, who only a year before had been accepting welfare from the country to keep his family alive, outmaneuvered Baer to win in a 15-round decision that left the boxing world in a state of shock. That was on June 13, 1935. For the next two years he toured the country making vaudeville appearances, radio program guest shots, and giving exhibition bouts.

Schmeling was still a top contender, and he demanded a chance at the crown. Braddock, who knew he was past his prime, decided to take on instead a young Negro, Joe Louis, figuring that since he was going to lose anyway it would hurt less to have the title remain in the United States.

Over 45,000 fans paid $715,470 to see the Champion make a good showing in the first round, only to be outpointed by Louis until knocked cold in the eighth round. It all happened in Comiskey Park in Chicago on June 22, 1937.

Instead of retiring as he announced at first, Jim came back seven months later to win, again against the predictions of nearly every sportswriter in the country, against a younger opponent, Tommy Farr. It was Braddock's last official fight.

During World War II Braddock was a Captain in the Army Transportation Corps. Thereafter, until 1956, he conducted a business in North Bergen, New Jersey, dealing in marine equipment. He is still a member of Local 825 of the Operating Engineers Union, which handles all the shipping into New Jersey ports. His two boys and one daughter all married and moved from their home in North Bergen.

In 1935, World Heavyweight Champion. *Ring Magazine*

From left to right: Joe Louis and James J. Braddock with the new title holder, Cassius Clay. *UPI*

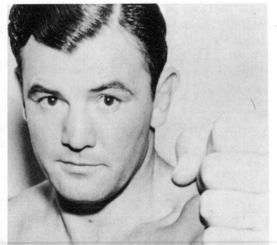

In 1930, after making the transition from silents to talkies.

LILA LEE

The silent screen star, whose real name was Augusta Appel, was born in New York City in 1901. One night when Lila was seven years old the famous producer David Belasco found her crying backstage in a theatre in Rochester, New York, because the Society for the Prevention of Cruelty to Children would not allow her to perform due to her age. He offered her his diamond watch to play with, and when she continued to cry he added his diamond stickpin and ring. Still she cried. Finally Belasco told her that when she was sixteen years old he would make her a star. Before she reached sixteen, however, after touring the country with the famous Gus Edwards' *School Days* vaudeville act, Lila was signed to a contract with Famous Players-Lasky Company which was soon to become known as Paramount Pictures. While with the vaudeville troupe she was called "Cuddles."

Her first major film, *The Cruise of the Make-Believe* (1918), was a smash. The next year Lila was in the Gloria Swanson starrer *Male and Female,* with Cecil B. de Mille as director. This was the cinema version of the classic *The Admirable Crichton* (a title some movie executive thought too toney). Other silent pictures include: *Blood and Sand* (1922) with the late Nita Naldi and Rudolph Valentino, *The Dictator* (1922) opposite Wallace Reid, *Broken Hearts* (1926), *New Klondike* (1926), *One Increasing Purpose* (1927), *Million Dollar Mystery* (1927), *You Can't Beat the Law* (1928), *Just Married* (1928), and *Black Butterflies* (1928).

Although Lila never enjoyed the same popularity in talkies, she worked right up until the late thirties in pictures such as: *The Show of Shows* (1929) with many stars of the silent period including Alice White (who resides in a house a block away from the Hollywood Bowl), *The Unholy Three* (1930) with Lon Chaney in his first and only talkie, *The Gorilla* (1930) with Walter Pidgeon, *Misbehaving Ladies* (1931) opposite Ben Lyon, *War Correspondent* (1932) in which her leading man was Jack Holt, father of Tim Holt, sales manager at a radio station in Oklahoma, *Night of June 13th*

(1932), *Face in the Sky* (1933) opposite Spencer Tracy, *The Ex-Mrs. Bradford* (1935) costarring with William Powell (who is semi-retired in Palm Springs, California), *The People's Enemy* (1935), and *Two Wise Maids* (1937) in which two of the screen's best remembered funnywomen appeared, Allison Skipworth and Polly Moran.

In the forties Miss Lee appeared in *Blind Alley* (1940) on Broadway and on the road, in *Claudia* (1941), and headed the Chicago company of *Kiss and Tell* (1943). Miss Lee had suffered three serious attacks of TB. The first in 1930 and then again in 1944 and 1946, thereafter living quietly and completely inactive.

In 1957 Ralph Edwards feted Lila on his *This Is Your Life* television program on NBC. A few of those who appeared on the show were Monte Blue; her ex-husband, James Kirkwood, who was also a silent film star; and her son James Kirkwood, Jr., who is a novelist, playwright, and actor. Unlike many of the stars who had paraded before the Edwards cameras, Lila was not there to plug a picture or a book. She had no idea she was to be the subject of the program, and was well deserving of the tributes paid to her.

In 1960 her son published a book which was both very funny and very sad about the life of a little boy whose mother is a beautiful screen actress. It was called *There Must Be a Pony*. Unfortunately, the stage production starring Myrna Loy was not as successful as the book, and never played in New York.

In 1964 Lila moved from New York City to Key West, Florida, and lives near her contemporaries Olga Petrova, who is in Clearwater, and Dorothy Dalton, who has a home in Lantana. Lila has not quite retired, having just done a television pilot in Florida.

Miss Lee came to New York recently for the opening of her son's play, *U.T.B.U.*, starring Tony Randall. The letters stand for Unhealthy to Be Unpleasant. Although the majority of reviews were favorable the production came at the time of a newspaper strike and lasted only a few weeks.

In retirement in Florida. *Poray Studio, Key West, Florida*

In a 1933 M-G-M publicity still.

JOHNNY WEISSMULLER

Until Johnny Weissmuller, who was to make a career out of playing Tarzan, came along, swimming was one of the most ignored sports in America. It was considered more an exercise than a competitive sport. "Big Johnny," as he was called, gave it glamour and excitement. He was six feet, three inches in height, and looked about as much like an Adonis as one could imagine. He had the kind of smile that city editors slap on the front pages rather than burying in the sports section. And to endear him further, he had an easygoing charm and sense of humor that won him friends among the press, the public, and even those who lost to him in competitions.

From 1921 until he turned professional in 1929 he won every free-style race he entered, an accomplishment never equaled or approached to this day. Under the sponsorship of the Illinois Athletic Club he swam on two Olympic teams and won five Gold Medals. In each of the five races he broke a world's record.

Of the 38 men's swimming records approved by the A.A.U. in 1922, 11 of them were Weissmuller's. He held the outdoor titles for the 100- and 400-yard races in 1922, 1923, and 1925 through 1928. In 1925 and 1927 he took the half-mile splash as well. In the Olympic races, in 1924 he won the 100-meter in 59 seconds and the 400-meter in 5 minutes 4.2 seconds, and in 1928 in Amsterdam he won the 100-meter in 58.6 seconds.

After appearing in a number of short sport films, he was spotted by scouts to make movies. In 1932 he made his first screen appearance in the role of Tarzan in *Tarzan, the Ape Man*. He made over a dozen feature films playing the Edgar Rice Burroughs character in such pictures as *Tarzan Escapes* (1936), *Tarzan's Desert Mystery* (1943), and *Tarzan and the Mermaids* (1948) with a number of leading ladies. One of the questions most frequently asked of the swimmer today is the whereabouts of the actor who played "Boy," Johnny Sheffield. (He lives with his wife and two sons in Santa Monica, California).

He made two feature films as another jungle hero, Jungle Jim: *Jungle Jim* (1949) and *Jungle Jim in the Forbidden Land* (1952). In 1958 his Jungle Jim series was a popular television show which was syndicated throughout the country. His only appearance in a movie other than as Jungle Jim or Tarzan was *Swamp Fire* in 1946.

Johnny, who was born in 1904, seldom misses a day's swim. He performed all of the stunts in his Tarzan films himself as well as one in which he rode a rhinoceros, a feat no animal handler or stunt man in Hollywood would undertake. At over sixty years of age he weighs 220 pounds and looks near forty.

Weissmuller has been married five times. His most famous wife was Lupe Velez, the Mexican actress, whose quarrels with Johnny made headlines. There were Camille Louier, Bobbe Arnst, a dancer, and Beryl Scott, a society girl. His last marriage was to the golf champion, Allene Gates.

Johnny's sense of humor has not always met with universal acceptance. Once during an Olympic swimming race in which he was not competing he and some of his teammates staged a comedy routine in the pool that had the judges in a rage and the audience in hysterics. A few years ago in Coral Gables, Florida, he failed to amuse the local authorities when he turned in a false fire alarm.

Since his movie days he has been vice-president of the Johnny Weismuller Swimming Pool Company, with headquarters in Chicago. Johnny commutes between the Windy City and his home in Fort Lauderdale, Florida.

Looking very tan and healthy in a recent photo. *John Virzi*

Sonja in 1940.

SONJA HENIE

The world's most famous ice skater was born in Oslo, Norway, in 1913. She began to skate when she was only seven years old and at eleven became the Figure Skating Champion of Norway. At thirteen she placed second in the World's Championships, and the next year, 1927, she won the title which she held for ten consecutive years.

Some of the records she set during her years as an amateur have yet to be equaled or broken. At the Winter Olympics held in St. Moritz, Switzerland, in 1928 Sonja won the Women's Figure Skating competition with 350.3 points. She repeated her victory at Lake Placid in 1932 with 328.94 points. She turned professional after taking the contest again in 1936 with 424.5 points in Garmisch-Partenkirchen, Germany.

Her first motion picture, *One in a Million* was released in 1937. The same year she made *Thin Ice* with Tyrone Power. Sonja Henie's films had musical numbers, handsome leading men, and her skating. They were very successful.

Her film credits include: *My Lucky Star* (1938) with Richard Greene, *Happy Landing* (1938), *Second Fiddle* (1939) opposite Rudy Vallee, *Everything Happens at Night* (1939) with Ray Milland, *Sun Valley Serenade* (1941) which was her best, costarring John Payne, *Iceland* (1942), *Wintertime* (1943) with Jack Oakie, and *It's a Pleasure* (1945). Her last movie was the remake of the 1934 Fay Wray (living in retirement in her home on Tigertail Road in West Los Angeles) starrer, *The Countess of Monte Cristo* (1948).

Even while making films Sonja found time to tour the United States and abroad with her ice revue. It was, in fact, the enormous financial success of the Henie ice shows that started the trend of frappé entertainment both in theatres and in arenas. The two biggest and oldest are Ice Follies and Ice Capades. Both shows have always been lavishly produced and have fared very well at the box office, but neither had Sonja Henie, nor anyone else of a comparable drawing power. Arthur Wirtz, who produced many of Sonja's shows, presented Barbara Ann Scott (married to an executive of the Merchandise Mart and proprietress of a beauty salon in the suburbs of Chicago) in his ice shows, and John H. Harris' Ice Capades featured his wife Donna Atwood (divorced from Harris and living with her three children in Los Angeles), but neither lady had the star quality possessed by the Norwegian skater. While both were excellent skaters and considerably younger than Miss Henie, they could never match her showmanship. Follies and Capades spent fortunes on acts and costumes that Sonja would never have permitted. However slow the rest of her show might have been, when the star skated onto the ice it would all but melt with that famous dazzling smile.

A typical year during her active period, 1942, saw her company gross $240,000 during an engagement at Madison Square Garden and over one million dollars on tour in addition to her movie money.

Much of the success of the famous Center Theatre in Rockefeller Center is attributed to Sonja Henie, whose shows there were very popular before it was turned into a TV studio. She played also at the now demolished Roxy Theatre, as well as Madison Square Garden and just about every arena in America. She has skated before crowned heads at Command Performances, on the "Ed Sullivan Show," and in 1956 on her own TV spectacular.

Sonja has been married three times. Her first husband was millionaire Dan Topping, her second was millionaire Winthrop Gardiner, Jr., and her present spouse is millionaire shipping magnate Nils Onstad, whom she married in 1956.

The Sonja Henie art collection is one of the most valuable accumulations of modern paintings in private hands. It includes Klees, Rouaults, Braques, Bonnards, and Matisses. When they were brought from Oslo, where they are kept, several years ago for a showing in Los Angeles, Sonja donated the proceeds of over $100,000 to the Heart Fund.

Miss Henie says that since her marriage she is no longer interested in touring and that "the ice seems so much colder these days." She does skate during her frequent stays in Switzerland and when she is living in her home in Norway. The Onstads divide their time between their native country and their big colonial house in Bel Air, California. Sonja, who is a national heroine in Norway, has received the Order of St. Olaf from the King.

Arriving at a recent Los Angeles première.

July, 1951, Heavyweight Champion of the World. *Wide World*

"JERSEY JOE" WALCOTT

The man who was to become the oldest prize fighter ever to hold the World's Heavyweight Championship and one of the most admired men in the ring was born in Merchantville, New Jersey, in 1914. His real name is Arnold Raymond Cream. He changed it when he turned professional in 1936 in honor of a famous welterweight from the early part of this century who was greatly admired by Walcott's father.

"Jersey Joe" grew up in a neighborhood where fighting was something every boy had to learn in order to survive. His parents had twelve children, and when his father died Joe, who was only fourteen, had to go to work to support the family. He sold newspapers, delivered groceries, and labored in a soup factory. Marrying at eighteen, he and his wife lived for eighteen months on a $9.50 home relief check when he couldn't find work. When he did manage to get another job it was as a hod carrier on a construction project, and finally as a longshoreman, to which he attributes his massive build and remarkable endurance.

For his first paid ring encounter he was given $7.50, winning the fight. Thereafter, when Joe fought regularly for money his record wasn't one of a future champion—he lost 15 of his 64 early fights because "hunger was a guest in my house,"though in 1936, while acting as a sparring partner for Joe Louis at the Champion's New Jersey training camp, he floored the great heavyweight in the first round.

On his way up the ladder Walcott beat some of the leading contenders around during the late thirties and forties. A few of those he either KO'd or beat by decisions were: Johnny Allen, Al Blake, Tommy Gomez, Jimmy Bivins, Lee Oma, Joe Maxim, and Elmer Ray. (Two of Walcott's matches before he had a shot at Louis' title were promoted by another New Jersey-ite, Frank Sinatra.)

When he finally met Louis officially in 1947 no one thought of him as a serious challenger until shortly after the first bell. To the amazement of everyone there the Champion hit the canvas twice in the first round, and was nearly knocked out in the seventh. Out of the 47 sportswriters who were present, 30 felt that the decision in favor of Louis was a raw one. Not since the famous Tunney "long count" has there been a more controversial outcome in a championship fight.

The Louis-Walcott rematch was held in Yankee Stadium on July 25, 1948. A record 42,667 people paid $841,739 to see the Champ KO Walcott in the eleventh round.

On June 22, 1949, Jersey Joe tried again for the Crown when he fought the new champ, Ezzard Charles (now a wholesale wine salesman in Chicago), but lost in a fifteen-round decision.

When he met Charles again in Pittsburgh on July 18, 1951, Walcott was thirty-seven years old. He had been beaten three times before in tries for the title, once by Charles. Then, during the seventh round, against all odds, Jersey Joe Walcott KO'd the Champion in front of 25,000,000 surprised TV viewers. When he was asked how he felt, the new Heavyweight Champion said, "I've worked twenty-one years for this night. I read my Bible before I fight. I prayed between every round. I asked God to help me."

Jersey Joe's only successful defense of his title was against Ezzard Charles in Philadelphia when he outpointed the former champion on June 5, 1952.

Four months later Rocky Marciano knocked Walcott out in the thirteenth round in Philadelphia. The gate was $504,645. Although he held the title for a short time, Joe's clean fighting in the ring and his gentlemanly behavior out of it earned him the admiration of the public and the respect of the professionals. In one of the world's most unsavory businesses Jersey Joe Walcott emerged as a winner at his sport while remaining faithful to his deep religious principles.

Since 1953 Walcott has worked with the Juvenile Division of the Camden, New Jersey, Police Department, and in 1965 was appointed Assistant Director of Public Safety. Always a family man, Joe seldom leaves Camden, where he lives with his wife and six children in a ten-room house, though he still finds time to spar with the local kids and teach Sunday school at the Methodist church in his hometown of Merchantville.

From left to right: Former Champs Jersey Joe Walcott, Joe Louis, and James J. Braddock with the new title holder, Cassius Clay. *UPI*

Starring in *Carmen, Jr.* in 1922 at the tender age of three.

BABY PEGGY

Baby Peggy's career began when she was only twenty months old. Her first efforts on the silent screen were two-reelers. Starting in 1920, she turned out over 150 of them. Peggy made feature-length films as well. Perhaps the best remembered of them is *Captain January* (1923), remade by Shirley Temple in 1936.

An indication of the popularity of the child star is evidenced in a 1923 advertisement placed in a trade paper by her studio, Universal Pictures. Of the four columns the studio bought, three of them were devoted to Baby Peggy's latest picture, *The Darling of New York*. Universal's classic *The Hunchback of Notre Dame* received one paragraph at the bottom of the advertisement. The headline as well as the photograph that accompanied the advertisement were about and of Baby Peggy.

All through the twenties Peggy toured the country as a vaudeville entertainer. Her act was so popular that years after she had retired an injunction was taken out by Peggy's parents to stop another child from performing under her name at the Chicago World's Fair of 1932. The impersonator was one of many.

In the mid-thirties Peggy emerged from her retirement on a Wyoming ranch to try a comeback in talkies as an ingenue. She gave up after a few small roles, and was little more than a curiosity in Hollywood during the sound era.

For a while Peggy was married to Gordon Ayres, who used to play Freckles in the silent version of *Our Gang* comedies. They were divorced at the end of World War II. (Ayres is now manager of the local Arthur Murray Dance Studio in Riverside, California. He ran unsuccessfully for Mayor in 1965.)

Peggy's real name was Peggy Montgomery. After divorcing Gordon she changed her Christian name to Diana. It was at this time that she was converted to the Roman Catholic faith. She is now known as Diana Serra Cary. The middle name is for the Spanish priest, Father Junipero Serra, who brought Christianity to Mexico and California. The surname of Cary was supplied by her present husband, artist Robert Cary, whom she married in 1954.

In 1957 the Carys moved from California to Cuernavaca, Mexico, where their son Mark was born in 1960. In 1966 the family moved to Spain where they now live, although their wish is eventually to settle in nearby Majorca.

Under the name of Diana Serra Cary the former star has published articles in *Esquire, Catholic Digest,* and *The Saturday Evening Post.* She is currently finishing her book on what she recalls from her years in motion pictures and vaudeville. Instead of the usual autobiography which recounts stories about famous silent stars who were her contemporaries, Peggy is concentrating mainly on the unknowns who made her era so outstanding. It will be a tribute to the cameramen, executives, character actors, and technicians who made ordinary men and women into idols of their time.

Another of Peggy's projects is the canonization of her patron, Father Serra. In the current campaign to elevate the Spaniard to sainthood, Peggy is in charge of public relations.

Of the past, Baby Peggy says, "As a child I enjoyed picture work, but not as an adult. I suffered emotionally from the stresses and strains of growing up in the limelight, but I have long since passed through the period of crisis. And I bypassed it not through the usual route of alcohol, love affairs, and self-pity. My religion has been the decisive factor in my happiness today, just as psychoanalysis has helped other child stars.

"Occasionally, even here people find out that I was once a child star. But the name confuses them, and they say, 'So this is whatever happened to Baby Jane!' "

With baby Mark in Cuernavaca recently.

Ursula Bernath

Heavyweight Champion
of the World, 1933.

PRIMO CARNERA

The Italian giant who became the Heavyweight Champion of the World was born in a town outside Venice in 1907. He left home at fourteen and traveled to France where he worked as a carpenter's apprentice and as a strong man in a circus. The veteran French heavyweight, Paul Journée, noticed Carnera's 6-foot 5¾-inch frame moving a piece of furniture with ease one day in the street, and got the idea of training him for the ring.

During 1928 and 1929 he ran up a rather impressive record fighting all over the Continent. In December, 1929, American promoters brought Carnera to the United States in a blaze of publicity that would have done credit to Barnum. He was taken all over the country and matched with opponents who were either aging or hopelessly outreached by the mammoth boxer. While the sportsmanship of this period in his career is questionable, the showmanship was superb.

On October 12, 1931, Jack Sharkey defeated him in Ebbets Field. But Primo turned right around and beat King Levinsky in Chicago, and then knocked out Argentine giant Vittorio Campolo, proving he had something more than size.

The first half of 1932 saw an impressive list of wins for Carnera all over Europe with the exception of his surprise defeat by ring veteran Larry Gains. He returned in July for another barnstorming tour, in which he defeated everyone put in front of him with the exception of Stanley Poreda. In most cases, however, he was meeting a man who had been carefully chosen to make the big boy look very good.

Then on February 10, 1933, he fought Ernie Schaaf in Madison Square Garden. Schaaf's performance was worse than anyone thought him capable of, and a blow that felled him in the 13th round did not seem to be a hard one. When Schaaf went down the crowd yelled "fake," and the sportswriters echoed the chant the next day in the papers. Three days later, the entire boxing world, and in particular those who had accused the Italian of a "fix," was shocked when Schaaf died of the results of that punch.

On June 29, 1933, Carnera took the Heavyweight title away from Jack

Sharkey by a knockout, and followed up his victory by whipping Paulino Uzcundun in Rome and then aging Tommy Loughran in Miami. Also in 1933 he made a movie called *The Prizefighter and the Lady* which had in the cast Max Baer, Jack Dempsey, Myrna Loy, and Walter Huston.

The Champion was favored when he stepped into the ring with Max Baer the night of June 14, 1934. Over 52,000 fans paid $428,370 to see one of the most exciting fights in ring history, with Baer flooring Carnera ten different times before the referee finally stopped the fight in the 11th round. He outweighed Baer by over 50 pounds and actually won several rounds, but Baer was the superior boxer.

Carnera remained a factor in boxing for a full year after losing the title. He KO'd Ray Impellitiere in early 1935, but Joe Louis ended his hopes for a comeback when the Brown Bomber flattened him in the 6th round on June 25, 1935. He returned to Europe in 1936 after losing a few more fights, only to find that he fared no better on the Continent. By 1937 his name had vanished from the news completely.

In 1939 he was in Yugoslavia on a public appearance tour, when he met his future wife, Pina, then a postmistress. The ex-Champion eked out a living by appearing at the openings of stores and movies in Southern Europe. During the War he fought in the Italian underground until he was captured and interned. He was released by Allied forces after Italy surrendered in 1944.

He then returned to this country as a wrestler. He did well enough at his second chance in the ring to buy a mansion in Italy, some forest land, a farm, and several houses, which he rents. In 1956 Humphrey Bogart starred in *The Harder They Fall,* a thinly veiled account of the career of Primo Carnera. It was Bogart's last film, and featured Mike Lane in the role of the giant prizefighter.

Although Primo isn't bitter, he does regret allowing people to take advantage of him when he was boxing. After that career was over he had no money—even after making as much as $122,000 in a single match. He is sorry also that he continued boxing after Louis beat him. Although he stopped wrestling several years ago, he has managed to keep his weight to just about what it was when he was Champion, 265 pounds. In addition to his holdings abroad, he prospers today as the proprietor of an Italian delicatessen and liquor store in Glendale, California. The Carneras have a married daughter and a son who is studying medicine.

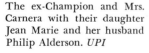

The ex-Champion and Mrs. Carnera with their daughter Jean Marie and her husband Philip Alderson. *UPI*

GERALD P. NYE

The highly controversial Senator has been called many things during his tenure in office from anti-Semite to dangerous appeaser, from reactionary to liberal. Domestically he could accurately be described as an old-fashioned agrarian rebel and internationally as a consistent isolationist.

Gerald Prentice Nye was born in Hortonville, Wisconsin, in 1892. He was, until appointed to a Senate vacancy in 1928, a crusading editor of a North Dakota newspaper which backed Robert La Follette's presidential bid in 1924. After being appointed by the Governor of North Dakota, Nye had to wait a full month while the Senate debated whether or not a governor had this power. After being backed by the powerful Senators, Norris and Borah, Nye was confirmed by a majority of two votes and took his seat. His appearance was described at the time as "an Old Oaken Bucket haircut and bulbous yellow shoes."

Several months later Nye ran in the regular election and won a full term. He chaired what was until then an obscure committee, the Public Lands Committee. Shortly after Nye took it over, his investigation into the financial dealings of Harry F. Sinclair and Andrew Mellon proved very embarrassing to both millionaires, and shook the structure of the Republican National Committee. The exposure for the first time gave him headlines he did not have to write, and from then on his career figured prominently in the news of the day.

Nye was a fighter from the very beginning of his political career. He fought for farm relief and against the World Court. He fought President Coolidge over North Dakota patronage, and won. The Baltimore *Sun* called him "Gerald, the Giant Killer."

In the Democratic landslide of 1932, Republican Nye was reelected by a ratio of 3 to 1. The new President, F.D.R., was a liberal, and since Nye hadn't liked Hoover or Coolidge many observers expected the Senator to fall into the fold of the New Deal. Instead Nye called the blue eagle symbol of the National Recovery Act "a bird of prey on the masses." When Hugh Johnson in 1933 invited him to join the board of the National Recovery Administration he declined.

In 1934 Nye carried on one of the most highly publicized investigations of the decade when he examined the munitions industry in this country, and created a sensation in the press which proved to be an embarrassment to J. P. Morgan. The general consensus about the effects among liberals was that they revealed the arms industry as a menace to world peace.

In 1935 the North Dakota Senator drafted the neutrality law forbidding arms shipments to belligerent nations, and in 1939 helped defeat F.D.R.'s attempts to remove the embargo. In 1940 Nye was seated on the Senate Foreign Relations Committee, affording him a perfect opportunity to fight the President tooth and nail on foreign policy.

The image of Nye during his public years is blurred by the seemingly inconsistent statements he made as well as the stands he took—in 1939 the German-American Bund cheered his name because he had called England "the greatest aggressor in modern times," whose "impending doom ought not to alarm us." Yet, that same year, he endorsed the controversial film *Confessions of a Nazi Spy* saying that propaganda from Hitler was just as dangerous as that from England. In early 1941 he lashed out against anti-Nazi films noting that they were made by an industry that was controlled mostly by foreigners and Jews. He confirmed the statement of Colonel Charles Lindbergh that people of the Jewish faith were leaders in the movement toward war, and encouraged Lindy to run for Congress. Nye opposed aid to the Soviet Union in 1940 stating that the country was ruled by "thieves, human butchers, and murderers of religion." He opposed the draft, lend-lease, the Great Lakes-St. Lawrence River development.

An accomplished speaker, Nye addressed such diverse movements as America First and the American League Against War and Fascism and on December 7, 1941, delivered an anti-war speech before 2,000 American Firsters. When he was told that Japan had bombed Pearl Harbor he said, "just what Britain planned for us. We have been maneuvered into this by the President [F.D.R.]." The next day he voted in the Senate to declare war.

Nye was defeated for reelection in 1945 and assumed the position of president of Record Engineering, Inc., in Washington, D.C. In 1959 he became Special Assistant for Elderly Housing in the Federal Housing Administration, resigning in 1963 for an appointment to the professional staff of the Senate Committee on Aging. He retired from government services in 1966, with a party given him by Senate Minority Leader, Everett Dirksen.

Nye lives with his wife in Chevy Chase, Maryland, and maintains an office in Washington, D.C., as a "consultant agent." He ardently supported Senator Goldwater in 1964 and approves of Medicare so long as it is economically feasible. The former Senator is very concerned over the fiscal policies of the present administration: "The frightening degree of inflation which has destroyed the values the old folks had laid away, or provided with retirement and/or insurance, leaves our country with poverty where adequate provision for rainy days had been made during productive years."

With famed criminal lawyer Clarence Darrow *(right)*; Nye at the time was Chairman of the National Recovery Review Board. *Acme*

At a recent Washington party
Chris Albertson

Flash Gordon getting out of another scrape in one of the chapters made in 1936. Dale is played by Jean Rogers.

LARRY "BUSTER" CRABBE

Paramount Pictures signed Buster after he won the 400-meter race in the 1932 water Olympics. He finished in 4 minutes and 48 seconds compared with Johnny Weissmuller's 1924 victory of 5 minutes and 4 seconds. His first pictures for Paramount were in a loincloth: *Tarzan the Fearless* (1933), and *King of the Jungle* (1933).

Although Buster made over 30 feature films during the thirties and forties as *Billy the Kid* and a 13-chapter serial of *Buck Rogers,* his public image will always be "Flash Gordon." The two serials he made portraying the earthman who battles Ming the Merciless became so popular that they were the first and only serials ever to be shown at evening performances in first-run houses. Eventually the chapters were put together and released as two feature films. Twenty years later, they were a hit all over again on television.

In the early fifties his *Captain Gallant of the French Foreign Legion* was a success as a syndicated television series. Appearing with Buster was his son Cuffy Crabbe who played his ward.

Buster had an early morning exercise show for a while during the fifties which emanated from New York City. He still appears from time to time as a guest on a TV show, and has done parts in westerns made by his old friend Eddie Small, the movie producer.

Since the early sixties Buster has been the aquatic director of the Hotel Concord in New York's Catskill Mountains. He likes to tell a story about his climbing out of the pool one day and overhearing one lady guest say to another, "Do you see that man? My dear, I remember him when I was a little girl. He used to play Flash Gordon." "I didn't mind it so much," says Buster, "except that I swear both of those gals were older than I am."

Buster is a grandfather by his daughter, whom he often visits in Los Angeles. Cuffy is now a student at a university in Arizona and his parents live in Rye, New York. Although "Ming the Merciless" (Charles Middleton) and "Dr. Zarkov" (Frank Shannon) are dead, he still keeps in touch with the lovely "Dale" (Jean Rogers) who is married to a top Hollywood agent.

Buster, who considered a career in law before he became successful as an actor, has done very well with his company, the Buster Crabbe Swimming Pools, which are very popular in the suburbs. Another of his business interests is his boys' camp in the Catskills. Buster recently joined a New York City stock brokerage firm as a licensed representative.

Unlike many stars who deeply resent being associated with one character, Crabbe delights in the revivals of Flash Gordon. Unlike most of the serials at that time, it was made on a budget of over $300,000 which in the thirties was more than some features cost. Buster is rightfully proud of his part in the series.

The fan mail still pours in from around the world where Flash Gordon is playing in theatres and on television. Most of it lately has been from the new African nation of Ghana. All the envelopes have to say is "FLASH GORDON, U.S.A."

"Buster" Crabbe, director of water sports at The Concord, Kiamesha Lake, N.Y.

Gene with his famous horse, Champion, on his Sunday night show in 1940. *CBS Radio*

GENE AUTRY

Gene Autry is one movie cowboy who really was a westerner by birth and upbringing. Born in Texas in 1907 he later moved to Sapulpa, Oklahoma, where he worked as a telegrapher at the local railroad junction. It was during that time when he was in his late teens that he got an additional job singing on the local radio station. One of his admirers was another Oklahoman, Will Rogers, who encouraged him to continue as an entertainer.

Gene became so popular in Oklahoma that within three years the radio show was his own and was being heard in several adjoining states. Columbia Records gave him a contract, and he was off to the races with his first hit which he also co-authored, "That Silver-Haired Daddy of Mine."

In 1933 he left radio for a while to make movies, his first with Ken Maynard in *In Old Santa Fe*. His 13-chapter serial *The Phantom Empire* (1934) is a classic of its type, and is still shown among devotees of the macabre in early sound films. He made over 64 feature films for Republic Pictures (which was still called Mascot Pictures when he made his first for them, *Tumblin' Tumbleweeds* in 1935).

Gene was the first western star to show up among the Top Ten moneymakers in Hollywood. He remained in those ranks from 1937 until 1942. He was also the first star to allow his name to be associated with merchandise, and has had as many as 100 different products on the market at one time bearing his name and likeness. Another first in Autry's life was in 1950 when he became the first cowboy to be named as one of the ten best dressed men in America.

His coast-to-coast radio shows for Wrigley Gum enjoyed great popularity, beginning in 1940. Listeners were always told that Gene was speaking to them right from Melody Ranch, and that his horse, Champion, was right there with him. Actually, Gene does live on a ranch in the San Fernando Valley called Melody Ranch.

His radio and movie work were halted from 1942 until 1945 when he served in the United States Air Force, from which he emerged a Flight

Officer. After the war he went back to work for Wrigley on Sunday nights and formed his own independent film company, for which he was to make 46 features.

During the years Gene reigned supreme as the screen's top cowboy, his formula set the pace for many other westerns. Any Autry fan will tell you that his pictures had ample comedy relief in the person of Smiley Burnette and the tops in western ballads, such as "South of the Border." There was, however, very little dalliance with girls. If the hero found it absolutely necessary to kiss the lady it would usually come in the last scene, and even then during the clinch the camera would pan to Champion, who looked about as uncomfortable as Gene wiping off the lipstick at the fade-out.

A musical group called "The Sons of the Pioneers" supplied the backing for Gene's numbers in many of his features. A young man appearing as a member of the group, and who later became "The King of the Cowboys," was Roy Rogers.

He had married Ina Mae Spiney in 1932, niece of his first song-writing collaborator.

Some of the songs he has introduced are "Mexicali Rose" and "Here Comes Santa Claus," both of which have sold over one million copies. His rendition of "Rudolph the Red-Nosed Reindeer" brought him a platinum copy after the sales went to two and one half million records.

Gene began devoting all of his time to his investments around the early fifties. He is Chairman of the Board of Golden West Broadcasting which controls radio station KVI in Seattle, KSFO in San Francisco, and KMPC in Los Angeles. In 1964 his corporation bought KTLA, Channel 5 in Los Angeles, from Paramount Pictures.

Autry's other interests and holdings include the Continental Hotel on Hollywood's Sunset Strip, the Mark Hopkins Hotel on Nob Hill in San Francisco, 25 percent interest in one music publishing firm and 100 percent in another, a flying school, a crop-dusting service, several ranches, several oil wells, the Gene Autry Championship Rodeo shows, and Gene Autry Television Productions which has produced such series as *Annie Oakley, Range Rider,* and *Buffalo Bill, Jr.*

Chairman of the Board of Golden West Broadcasting.

In the prime of her career, in *Dragonwyck*, 1946, directed by Ernst Lubitsch, and *(below)* today.

ANNE REVERE

She has been playing old women so long that most of her fans expect her to be ancient. Anne was born in 1903 in New York City and attended Wellesley College. During the twenties she worked throughout the United States in stock and repertory.

In 1931 she made her debut on Broadway in *The Great Barrington* and then *Lady With a Lamp* the same year, appearing the next season in *Wild Waves*. In 1933 she did the play *Double Door* in New York, leaving for Hollywood to film the screen version released in 1934, starring Evelyn Venable (married to cinematographer Hal Mohr and teaching Greek at U.C.L.A.). It was Miss Revere's first motion picture and her last for six years.

In 1934 Lillian Hellman's play *The Children's Hour* was presented on Broadway with Miss Revere in the role of Martha Dobie. The theme was very controversial for the time. It was the first time a production had dealt openly with the subject of Lesbianism, and it was an enormous success. Anne's personal reviews established her as one of the top character actresses in the New York theatre. After its Broadway run she took the play on tour.

In 1937 she played Celia in *As You Like It*, and in 1939 was one of *The Three Sisters* on Broadway.

In 1940 Anne Revere was brought back to Hollywood where she made one movie after another for the next 19 years. A few of those films, which were distinguished by her performances, are: *The Howards of Virginia* (1940), *Men of Boys Town* (1941), *Flame of New Orleans* (1941), the memorable Bette Davis-Miriam Hopkins starrer, *Old Acquaintance* (1942), *The Keys of the Kingdom* (1944), *Dragonwyck* (1946), *Forever Amber* (1947), *Body and Soul* (1947), and *You're My Everything* (1949).

Miss Revere has been nominated for the Best Supporting Actress Oscar on three occasions, winning it once: her performance as Jennifer Jones's mother in *The Song of Bernadette* (1943), her role in *National Velvet* (1945), and her portrayal of Gregory Peck's mother in *Gentleman's Agreement* (1947). She won the statuette in 1945.

126

In 1951 the actress turned in another splendid performance as the mother of Montgomery Clift in *A Place in the Sun,* the last motion picture audiences ever saw her in. Anne Revere's name was one of the 300 that appeared on the Hollywood Blacklist. Although, unlike her friend and neighbor, Gale Sondergaard, she has been able to find occasional TV work and parts in Broadway plays, the actress who was once one of the highest paid and most respected character people in films is still *persona non grata* in that medium. It seemed the heads of the major studios determined that Anne Revere was no longer suitable for employment in their industry.

For a time after Hollywood had found her political associations not to its liking, she and director Samuel Rosen (her husband since 1935) ran an acting school in Los Angeles. In the late fifties the couple returned to New York City and bought a brownstone on West 104th Street, which has all of the original woodwork and fixtures of its first owner, William Burns, of detective agency fame.

Since her blacklisting she has been seen on Broadway both in Elmer Rice's unsuccessful modernization of *Hamlet* entitled *Cue for Passion* in 1958, and in *Jolly's Progress* in 1959. When Anne was given the role of one of the sisters in *Toys in the Attic* the rumor was that Lillian Hellman, the author, had chosen her merely because of their association in 1934. The fact is, the actress originally signed for the part did not work out, and though Miss Revere was a second choice, she received the Antoinette Perry Award in 1960 for her performance.

On TV, the only major roles Anne has had were in 1960 when she was seen in *The House of Bernarda Alba* and in a one-act Tennessee Williams play presented in 1961. (She had appeared in a televised drama as far back as 1939.)

Anne has kept busy over the past few years acting in plays at colleges and universities around the country. Since 1965 she has appeared from time to time in a running part on ABC Television's *A Time for Us,* a daytime soap opera. When she signed the contract she refused to comment to interviewers on her blacklisting other than to say, "I've talked about it until I am tired of hearing myself, and I expect those listening are tired too. I am very glad to be back working and hope to continue."

ABC

Irene and Vernon Castle, 1917.
Dance Magazine

IRENE CASTLE

It was a handsome young couple, named Vernon and Irene Castle, who changed the style of dancing in this country before the First World War, as much by their personalities as by the steps they created. They were the most idolized pair in America, and the dances they introduced, such as the "Castle Walk" and "Castle Waltz," became absolute crazes in ballrooms in every city and town. (While appearing in Chicago they danced "The Castle Walk" down the aisle at the city's first "tango wedding" while a couple named Florence Eizendrath and L. Montefiore Stein were united in holy matrimony.)

The greatest influence, however, that Irene Castle had on her time was not a dance or a theatrical innovation but a coiffure. She did what no other woman of that period would have dared to do and still keep her reputation —she bobbed her hair. Overnight the style became respectable, if still a bit "daring."

In the year 1914 at the pinnacle of their career the Castles were drawing an average of $31,000 a week doing one-night stands and during their fame were the proprietors of a cabaret called Sans Souci. When Madison Square Garden held an amateur dancing tournament the Castles, as the most famous and admired married couple in the country, sponsored it, assuring its success by the magic of their names alone.

It was not a change in trends or a loss of popularity that ended the Castle legend. In 1915, Vernon, who had always been an enthusiastic supporter of England, was accepted into the Royal Canadian Flying Corps as a second lieutenant. After shooting down two German planes he was promoted to the rank of Captain. In 1917 he was sent to Canada to train pilots, and when America entered the war he was transferred to Texas to do the same for American aviators. In February of 1918 Castle was killed in an air crash during a training flight.

Irene Castle continued after Vernon's death to set fashions in hair styles, clothing, and dances in films and on the stage. They had made silent films together such as *Whirl of Life* (1915) and appeared on the stage in *Watch Your Step* (1915). Alone, Irene had great success on the stage and screen both during the war when her husband was away and after she had been widowed. On Broadway she costarred with Vivienne Segal (now retired with the exception of an occasional TV appearance in southern California) in *Miss 1917*. She starred in featured films such as *The Hillcrest Mystery* (1918) and an extremely popular serial of the day, *Patria* (1917), in which she was billed as "the most popular and admired woman in America," and throughout the twenties she was a popular figure in vaudeville.

Although Irene Castle had become less active by the thirties, her popularity was sufficient to set gate records when the New York World's Fair of 1939 honored her with an Irene Castle Day. She rose to the occasion by creating the "New York World's Fair Hop."

Little has been heard of the once famous dancer since then. Most of her time and energy have been devoted to her favorite cause, a sanctuary for stray pets. From her large beautiful home in Lake Forest, Illinois, Irene operates a shelter (which she calls "Orphans of the Storm") for any and all breeds.

Dance Magazine feted her with a birthday party in New York City in one of her rare public appearances in recent years, attended by such luminaries as Bette Davis, Pearl S. Buck, and Marge and Gower Champion. Said Miss Castle, who was born in 1893, "I could have danced all night."

At her seventy-first birthday party. *Dance Magazine*

In *Thrill of a Lifetime* with Ben Blue, 1937.

JUDY CANOVA

Judy Canova, who made a career of being a hillbilly, began life in 1916 in Jacksonville, Florida. She was part of a family vaudeville team until 1934 when she landed a part in the Broadway show *Calling All Stars* with Gertrude Niesen (who now lives in retirement in Los Angeles).

Her big break came the following year in Hollywood when director Busby Berkeley gave her a bit without billing in *In Caliente*. The popular singer of the day, Wini Shaw (now living in Sunnyside, Long Island, with her husband, a box office treasurer of a New York theatre), was to sing "The Lady in Red" in a nightclub scene, and Berkeley created one of his most beautiful and extravagant production numbers around it. Just as it ended, from behind a pillar Judy appeared in a costume resembling Wini Shaw's. The moment she opened her mouth to sing all of the effect created by the original performance was destroyed. The audience howled. It is a wonder the song survived the Canova treatment to become a standard. (Thirty years later when the Gallery of Modern Art in New York City held a Busby Berkeley festival Judy's takeoff brought down the house once more.)

Judy immediately got other parts suited to her hillbilly hokum. Few knew that the absurd voice she used to butcher songs with had been trained for classical singing.

Her vignettes in important films such as *Thrill of a Lifetime* (1937) and *Artists and Models* (1937) were so popular that in the late thirties she began

130

to make what were known as "programmers." These were full-length films made on a low budget that played the lower half of double bills. A few that Judy turned out were: *Scatterbrain* (1940), *Puddin' Head* (1941), *Singing in the Corn* (1947), *Honeychile* (1951), *WAC from Walla Walla* (1952), and *Untamed Heiress* (1954).

From the war years and on into the fifties, long after many other popular radio shows had fallen by the wayside—with the advent of television—Judy had a popular weekly half-hour radio program. One of the characters appearing with her was called "Pedro." His expression, "Pardon me for talking in your face, *Señorita*," became a household remark during the forties. Another character introduced on the *Judy Canova Show* was her "Cousin Ureenus" who used to eat chopped liver ice cream. On signing off, Judy would sing the popular song "Goodnight Sweetheart."

Variety, which began reviewing television shows in 1939, credits Judy Canova's appearance that year as being the first hillbilly act ever seen on the medium. Judy formed her own TV production company, Caravan, Inc., in 1957 but has hardly been seen with the exception of some guest appearances on the *Huckleberry Finn Show* in the late fifties.

Judy makes an occasional rodeo appearance, though she doesn't have to work anymore and chooses her roles sparingly.

Those expecting to find Judy living in the Ozarks with chickens running around her front yard would be greatly surprised by her beautifully furnished home and tasteful clothes. She lives with her second husband, a real estate broker, and her daughters Diane and Julietta in the San Fernando Valley—not far from the retreat of the widow of Herbert Yates, longtime head of Republic Pictures. Vera Hruba Ralston, the Czech ice skater-actress, known to movie fans as the Queen of the "B's," lives with her mother and 17-year-old dog.

A sophisticated Judy today.

HELEN WILLS MOODY

The girl who grew up to be the world's greatest female tennis player was born in Centerville, California, in 1906. Her maiden name was Helen Newington Wills, but she was known by her married name after she and Frederick S. Moody, Jr., wed in 1929.

Her record stands to this day. She was the undisputed Queen of Tennis not only for her game but because she had that certain something that makes the difference between the great and the near-great. She wore her famous white visored hat like a crown. Her manner was cold and calculating toward her opponents and disdainful to the press and spectators. She was beautiful, and moved on and off the courts with the authority of a champion. Helen had star quality.

Her concentration on the game was absolute, and no matter what happened or how the crowd cheered, her expression remained impassive. In no time she had been dubbed "Little Miss Poker Face."

Helen Wills Moody was the winner of the United States Women's Singles in 1923, 1924, 1925, 1927, 1928, 1929, and 1931. She played on eight Wightman Cup teams, winning 18 singles against 2 losses. She shared the United States Women's Doubles victories in 1922, 1924, 1925, and 1928.

At Wimbledon, England, where the international games are played, she won the singles eight years: 1927, 1928, 1929, 1930, 1932, 1933, 1935, and 1938, and with various partners took the doubles there in 1924, 1927, and 1930.

Helen was the victor of the French Singles four times. Her most dramatic appearance there was against the great French player, Suzanne Lenglen. The press in the United States, while rightfully proud of her, whipped the nation up to fever pitch over the match by playing on national pride, making the contest into something resembling good versus evil. Miss Lenglen and her American opponent were as different as night and day. Lenglen drank, smoked, was seen constantly in Riviera nightclubs, and was unattractive. The foreign newspapers, on the other hand, saw the Frenchwoman as chic, which she was, and fun-loving. Helen Wills Moody appeared to them to be humorless, virginal, and far too sure of herself. It was close to a national tragedy when "our Helen," as the press called her in those days, was trounced 6–3 and 8–6.

It is a great pity that such a splendid career was marred by her rather petulant behavior. A very unfortunate incident lingers in the memories of tennis fans from the Women's National Singles of 1934, which were held at Forest Hills. Mrs. Moody had beaten Helen Hull Jacobs each time they had met, the latter always taking it very well. This time Miss Jacobs had achieved one set up and had a big lead in the second when Mrs. Moody, complaining of an injured spine, defaulted the set, match, and championship by walking off the court. Although she did have an operation after that and was away from her game for a year, rumor had it that the very next day she had to be talked out of playing in the doubles by her partner because the default of the previous day would have been pounced

132

on by the press as merely an act of female pettiness in denying her old opponent the satisfaction of a clear-cut victory.

The following year at Wimbledon, Helen Jacobs came within a breath of that victory until Mrs. Moody turned the tables in the last minutes of the finals and took the title.

Mrs. Moody has written two books, *Tennis,* which she also illustrated, in 1928, and "15–30," which was published in 1937, a year before she retired from major tournament play.

She has never commented publicly about the remarks made about her in the autobiography of the late Bill Tilden, tennis' greatest male player. If only a portion of what he related about her personality in *My Story* is true it would explain why Helen Wills Moody is remembered most, while Helen Jacobs is remembered best.

She married her second husband, Aidan Roark, in 1939 and for a while they lived in Pacific Palisades, California. They now reside in one of the most beautiful communities on the West Coast, Carmel-by-the-Sea, California, a small wooded community of wealthy residents right on the Pacific Ocean. Mrs. Roark is as aloof in retirement as she was while in the public eye. Her attitude toward her game these days seems puzzling. She does not appear at tournaments or keep in touch with players. The United States Lawn Tennis Association has never been notified that she and her husband moved a number of years ago to her present address. Also, it has been years since she subscribed to *World Tennis* magazine or communicated with them. About the only activity she participates in is Republican politics.

Helen Wills Moody in a photograph taken before her famous match with Helen Hull Jacobs at Forest Hills in 1934. *U.S. Lawn Tennis Association.* With dog "Docky," at her home in California recently (*right*). *UPI*

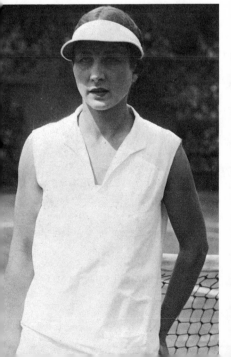

ANNA STEN

The famous actress' real name is Anjuchka Stenska. She was born in Russia in 1910, the daughter of a Swedish mother and a Russian ballet master. She worked as a waitress at the age of twelve, soon after her father died.

When she was fifteen the great Stanislavsky saw her in an amateur play in Kiev and arranged for her to enter the Moscow Film Academy. At eighteen she was part of a traveling troupe doing plays throughout Russia under the auspices of the Moscow Art Theatre. At first she made Russian films in the Crimea and then at the big studios in Moscow. Anna then was sent to Germany to make pictures on a German-Russian coproduction arrangement. Two of the movies she made in Russia are perfect examples of the excellent work turned out at the time by the Soviet cinema, *Girl with the Hatbox* (1927) and *The Yellow Ticket* (1928).

Anna Sten played opposite the late Anton Walbrook in the talkie *Trapeze* (1931) which had as its director the great German talent, E. A. Dupont. Another of her better pictures of that period in Germany was *Bombs Over Monte Carlo* (1931). It was, however, her part of Grushenka in *The Brothers Karamazov* (1931) that brought her to the attention of the American producer Samuel Goldwyn. The film was directed by a Russian, Fedor Ozep, who was also her husband. Before accepting Goldwyn's five-year contract she and Ozep parted, and in 1932 Anna married her present husband, the producer of *Karamazov,* Eugene Frenkes.

Anna Sten arrived in Hollywood in 1932. When she first drove down Hollywood Boulevard she thought it so strange that it must be all one large movie set.

Her first film was not released until 1934. The two-year interim was used by Goldwyn to have his new star tutored in English while he was making her the subject of one of the most intensive personal publicity campaigns Hollywood had ever seen.

Nana opened in New York's Radio City Music Hall on February 1, 1934. Her leading man was Phillips Holmes, whom Goldwyn borrowed from Paramount. The sets were lavish and Miss Sten was beautiful. Her screen debut was directed by Dorothy Arzner, one of the hottest in the business at that time. Miss Arzner faded from pictures several years later and is now directing television commercials in Los Angeles. The picture received good notices but did not fare well at the box office.

Goldwyn had originally promised Anna that he would do an American version of *The Brothers Karamazov.* Instead he gave her a production of another Tolstoy novel *Resurrection* which was called on the screen *We Live Again* (1934). Opposite her was one of the screen's most popular actors, Fredric March. Again Goldwyn spared no expense, and again the film flopped dismally at the box office.

Her third and final effort under that contract was with Gary Cooper in *The Wedding Night* (1935). It is Anna's favorite among her American

134

movies. The picture had star names, a top production, good release, publicity, and reviews. The only thing wrong was, like the other two, nobody went to see it. The Goldwyn-Sten contract was dissolved by "mutual agreement."

Miss Sten made other films during the thirties and forties both in Hollywood and England, but none of them were great successes. In each, however, *Exile Express* (1939), *They Came to Blow Up America* (1943), and *Three Russian Girls* (1944), she was a joy to look at and turned in a good performance.

Anna Sten has been referred to as "Goldwyn's Folly" and "The Edsel of the Movie Industry." Whatever the reason for her failure to click with the public, she was indisputably a fine actress and a classic beauty. Most movie historians feel that she was oversold and improperly handled.

Miss Sten maintains both a ranch-style house in Beverly Hills and an apartment in New York City. During the war she began painting and has had one-woman shows in Los Angeles and New York which were critically and financially successful. Her first show in Los Angeles in 1962 sold out completely. Her works were sent on a European tour by the Smithsonian Institution and are in the collection of the Boston Museum.

With the exception of an English picture *The Nun and the Sergeant* (1962) and an occasional TV role Anna Sten devotes most of her time to painting. When she is in New York, however, she attends classes at the Actors Studio and promises to appear in a play for them if it is produced on Broadway. Her role in it: an Eskimo.

The Edsel of the movie industry in *Nana* for **Samuel Goldwyn, 1934.** A deeply suntanned Anna Sten in her Manhattan apartment recently *(right)*.

Alfred Monaco

About to give the downbeat for a 1945 CBS radio broadcast.

PHIL SPITALNY

The all-girl orchestra leader received his musical training in Eastern Europe, where he was born. His expertise as a conductor was obvious to vaudeville impresarios who gave him steady employment in the pits of their houses after he came to the United States. For a while he settled down in Cleveland, Ohio, at the Allen Theatre where in a short time he became a local favorite.

In the late twenties Spitalny conceived his idea for an all-girl orchestra. He had gone to hear the debut of a fourteen-year-old violinist named Evelyn Kaye. He was so taken by her playing that he immediately thought of hiring her. As she continued to play, the idea expanded. Why not lots of girl musicians? Why not all girls? Beautiful talented girls and lots of strings. The teenager was hired and performed simply under the name "Evelyn," but not for long, for soon fan mail began to pour in describing her technique as "magic." Thus she became the only musician ever to have her instrument receive equal billing, becoming known as "Evelyn and Her Magic Violin." As he envisioned his new orchestra, a vaudeville tour would be impractical because of its size. But this was the time of the new entertainment medium known as radio. In spite of the novelty of the group being essentially visual, the all-girl concept was a radio hit, and like most innovations it inspired a number of copies. Spitalny's orchestra, however, was never seriously challenged because of the quality of its sound. Most of the members were hand picked from Manhattan's famed Julliard School of Music.

One of the first sponsors of *The Hour of Charm,* as the show was called, was a national manufacturer of chocolate. The slogan of the product was

"Chocolate of the highest quality for the lowest price." These were the days of live radio. The announcer walked to the microphone and told audiences from coast to coast that the program was being brought to them by "Chocolate of the lowest quality for the highest price." The studio audience howled. Spitalny doubled in two. The girls giggled. But when the announcer was so convulsed he couldn't say it correctly, it was the last straw. The contract was immediately cancelled. Although there was another sponsor ready to pick up the tab, that was the last *Hour of Charm* with a male announcer. From then on Spitalny's music was introduced by "The Voice of Charm." One of the female announcers with the program for many years was Arlene Francis.

Although Phil Spitalny was famous throughout the land, none of his radio listeners knew that he spoke with a heavy accent. Throughout his career Phil never said a word on the air, until a 1965 interview.

In the late forties, when it seemed clear that television and not radio would be the dominant medium, Spitalny decided not to make the switch, remembering that he had always promised himself that when he had attained success he would know when to quit.

Phil Spitalny and Evelyn have been married since 1950 when they moved to Miami Beach. Their home was built to their specifications—it contains not only a music room but a bathtub shaped like a violin. One of their neighbors is the former movie beauty, Toby Wing, married to the famous pioneer aviator, Richard Merrill.

For a while Phil suffered ill health after his retirement. He has recovered and is now the music critic for the Miami Beach *Sun*. Every summer Phil and Evelyn come to New York on their way to the music festivals of Europe. During their stopover an annual luncheon of all the *Hour of Charm* girls who live in the area is held in the hotel where the Spitalnys stay.

With wife, Evelyn, at a recent opening in Miami Beach. *Allen Malschick*

"The Male Shirley Temple," during a 1937 appearance on *The Eddie Cantor Show.*

BOBBY BREEN

The child actor had been around even before Eddie Cantor made him a regular on the late entertainer's weekly radio show in 1936. It was, however, that exposure on coast-to-coast radio that made Bobby Breen a star. He became so identified with Cantor that when Bobby called him "Uncle Eddie" the public actually believed that he was a nephew. On the same shows with Breen was another Cantor discovery, a young lady who was to become one of Universal Pictures' biggest money-makers during the thirties, Deanna Durbin. Now married to a film director, Miss Durbin lives in Paris shuddering at even the mention of a comeback.

In the thirties every major lot in Hollywood had a child star. RKO had Bobby. From the age of eight until his voice began to change he made films such as *Hawaii Calls* (1938), *Fisherman's Wharf* (1939), and *Way Down South* (1939). As a child star he was made conscious of budgets, overtime, bookings, grosses, etc. He had a fortune put aside for him before he was grown up, a name that is still recognized around the world, and the experience of a veteran entertainer. To Bobby, he was a boy who had everything but a childhood.

With short pants, curly hair, and a soprano voice Breen forged a sissified image that has haunted him through his service in the United States Army, two marriages, and his second career as an adult singer in nightclubs.

In his appearances today he peppers his act with songs such as "Rainbow on the River" (the title song from his 1936 motion picture). The voice is deeper now but it still has that same distinctive quality that made matrons want to cuddle him and kids want to kick him. "They expect me to come onstage still wearing short pants," says Bobby. "It takes a lot of work out there to make them believe I'm grown up. They resent it somehow. It's something I have to fight every single performance."

Breen considered several other professions after his discharge from the Army, and event spent some time in the real estate business, but show business was too much a part of him. Although the money he had made before the war was in trust waiting for him when he came of age, there remains a thinly veiled bitterness about those years, and he frankly admits that if his son were to choose a career in show business it would be a great disappointment to him.

When asked about some of his contemporaries Bobby says, "I dated Shirley Temple once, but it was only a publicity stunt. Cora Sue Collins came backstage to see me a couple of years ago when I was playing Houston, and it was nice to see her again. They tell me that Dickie Moore has an office in this building, but I never see him. I didn't see much of them even in those days. It wasn't that I didn't like them, but there just wasn't time."

Bobby Breen Productions maintains offices in the theatrical district of Manhattan booking Bobby's club act which has played Australia, New Zealand, and South Africa in recent years to excellent reviews.

Bobby's wife works closely with him, and they commute together daily from their Riverdale, New York, home. The most exciting item on the horizon for the Breens is the contract Bobby recently signed with Mo-Town Records. The Detroit firm handles some of the hottest names in Rock 'n' Roll, such as the Supremes. Breen's first record for them will be a Rock version of "Rainbow on the River."

Today as he appears in nightclubs around the world.
CBS Radio

A publicity shot taken during the 1930's at the height of his popularity on radio. *CBS Radio*

LANNY ROSS

Though not as a singer, Lanny Ross has been performing since the age of four. He began on the stage in London, and at six years was with the great actor George Arliss in his production of *Disraeli*. His own father was the well-known Shakespearean actor, Douglas Ross.

After attending Yale, receiving a degree, and being admitted to the New York Bar, Lanny decided to try his luck at singing. He had been a member of the famous "Whiffenpoofs" at Yale.

Lanny made his debut under the title "The Troubador of the Moon" on Christmas morning, 1928. His success was almost immediate and lasted longer than that of most of the singers who were overnight sensations on the infant medium, radio.

For six years he was the singing star of the Maxwell House *Show Boat*, emceed by the late Charles Winninger. Packard Motor Cars' *Mardi Gras* and Camel Cigarettes' *Camel Caravan* were two other important radio shows featuring his name during the thirties.

Lanny was as handsome and romantic-looking as he sounded over the air. In Hollywood he starred in *Melody in Spring* in 1934 opposite a young lady who had just changed her name from Harriet Lake, which is what it had been on Broadway, to Ann Sothern. His costars in *College Rhythm* (1934) were the late Joe ("You wanna buy a duck?") Penner and the lovely Helen Mack, who lives in the apartment next to Lanny's on Manhattan's East 57th Street. The feature-length Fleischer cartoon *Gulliver's Travels* (1939) featured the voices of Lanny Ross and his other neighbor, Jessica Dragonette.

In 1938 Lanny Ross was the featured male vocalist on the Lucky Strike *Hit Parade*. The top songs of the year were "Thanks for the Memory" and "Jeepers Creepers."

Throughout his career his theme "Moonlight and Roses" was the sign-off on all his network programs. Probably the most popular of all was his Monday through Friday Franco-American show immediately following *Amos 'n' Andy*.

During the Second World War Ross served on General Douglas MacArthur's staff in the South Pacific. He was later awarded the Medal of Merit.

In the early days of television Lanny had the popular *Swift's TV Variety Show* and *The Lanny Ross Show*.

Ross married Olive White, his press agent, in 1935. Their only child, a daughter, died a few years ago. In the living room of their duplex apartment are large portraits of their granddaughter and her late mother.

Lanny has taken up painting. One of his friends who encouraged him in his hobby and complimented him on his efforts is the wife of the famous art dealer, Victor Hammer, of the Hammer Galleries. She was for nearly thirty years one of the best loved women on radio, Ireene Wicker, "The Singing Lady."

Lanny Ross is active in the affairs of the radio and TV performers union, the American Federation of Television and Radio Artists, and is on the board of the scholarship fund named for the founder of the union, the George Heller Foundation.

Although he is less active before the cameras and microphones, Ross is quite well known as a producer of industrial shows. He also finds time to perform occasionally in summer stock and nightclubs around the country.

The main project taking up his time is a Broadway show which has been in the works for some time. Lanny has written the music and lyrics, and plans to have it produced under the title *Morning Town*.

Lanny is today a producer, a grandfather, and still a performer.   *Augusta Berns*

In 1942, when her "peek-a-boo" sweep was the rage of the country.

VERONICA LAKE

Veronica Lake was born Constance Ockleman in 1919 in Lake Placid, New York. Her father was a college professor and, before she decided on a theatrical career, she was a premedical student at McGill University.

In 1941 she was under contract to Paramount Pictures. There was a role for a beautiful girl in one of their big pictures of that year. Since the male stars, William Holden, Ray Milland, and Brian Donlevy, would provide enough star power to assure the picture's success, the front office decided to take a chance on their starlet with the peculiar hair-do. The film was *I Wanted Wings,* and Veronica was a sensation and a brand new exciting star. She introduced the "peek-a-boo" hair-do which swept the country's beauty parlors overnight. So popular, in fact, was this new coiffure that during World War II the Defense Department of the United States made an official request of Paramount to change the hair style of their star. So many women in defense plants had emulated it that there were countless work stoppages and injuries from hair getting caught in machines. She obliged by adopting another favorite style of the time, the upsweep.

Another 1941 movie that proved Miss Lake to be a skilled comedienne was *Sullivan's Travels.* She turned in a splendid performance opposite Joel McCrea, under Preston Sturges' direction. Veronica's hair was hidden under a man's cap during much of the film, demonstrating that she was more than just a girl with a gimmick.

In 1942 Paramount took another chance on a young actor under contract to them named Alan Ladd. They had difficulty casting him because he was extremely short. So was Veronica. Together they made *This Gun for Hire.*

142

From then on, half of the leading ladies in Hollywood would have walked in a trench all through a picture to meet the height requirements for playing opposite the dynamic new star. The magnetic combination of Lake and Ladd was seen in three other films: *The Glass Key* (1942), *The Blue Dahlia* (1946), and *Saigon* (1948).

Another smash for Veronica in 1942 was her role opposite Fredric March in *I Married a Witch*. The following year she was in the all-star *Star Spangled Rhythm* and *So Proudly We Hail,* a popular film about women at war which had Claudette Colbert and Paulette Goddard in the cast. She made two pictures with Eddie Bracken in 1945: *Out of This World* and *Hold That Blonde,* and one with Sonny Tufts (who lives in Hollywood and appeared on a special TV show in 1966 as the trivia personality of the year): *Bring on the Girls,* followed by another picture with Tufts, *Miss Suzy Slagle* (1946).

Some of her other credits include the excellent melodrama *Hour Before Dawn* (1944) with Franchot Tone, *Duffy's Tavern* (1945), and *Isn't It Romantic* (1948).

After she left Paramount in the late forties little was heard of her other than occasional stories about her personal life—none of which were pleasant though reportedly true. In 1951 she and husband André de Toth filed voluntary bankruptcy petitions and their $120,000 Hollywood home was seized for nonpayment of taxes. At its auction there were no bidders. Following the couple's divorce Veronica moved to New York City.

She worked for a while during 1962 as a hostess in the restaurant of the Martha Washington Hotel in New York and was for a short time in 1963 a waitress in a Greenwich Village café, thereafter drifting from one odd job to another. In 1964 she appeared off-Broadway in the revival of *Best Foot Forward.* She got fine notices, and the show was a hit, but the comeback that many believed and hoped for did not happen.

Veronica still lives in New York City, but grants very few interviews. She seems anxious to work, and has done some roles in Florida during the 1965–66 season, and a low-budget movie in Montreal recently. On her return she stopped in the Midwest to visit her new grandchild.

In a New York theatre lobby recently.

BURTON K. WHEELER

The influential isolationist Senator was born in Hudson, Massachusetts, in 1882, the son of a shoemaker. After attending public schools there, he went to the University of Michigan, graduating from the law school in 1905. That same year he opened a law office in Butte, Montana. He was elected to the Montana Legislature in 1910, appointed United States District Attorney in 1913, serving until 1918, was defeated for governor in 1920 but elected United States Senator in 1922, serving four terms until 1946.

Although elected to the Senate as a Democrat, a year later he switched party affiliations and ran on the Progressive Party ticket as the vice-presidential candidate with Robert "Fighting Bob" La Follette, the presidential candidate. They received 4,822,856 popular and 13 electoral votes.

He backed the Democratic candidate, Al Smith, in 1928 and was one of the earliest preconvention supporters in 1932 of the New York governor, Franklin D. Roosevelt, as well as being instrumental in obtaining for Roosevelt the support of Louisiana's powerful "Kingfish" Huey Long.

Throughout the first few years of Roosevelt's New Deal, the Montana Senator voted for most of its measures. He balked, however, at the far-reaching effects contained in the National Recovery Act. Wheeler's leeriness of the complicated bill was proved justified when it was later declared unconstitutional by the Supreme Court.

In 1937, when F.D.R. presented the Congress with his bill to pack the Supreme Court, Wheeler split with his party's leader saying that what the President was asking for amounted to dictatorial powers and the control of all branches of government. Up until that time Wheeler had always enjoyed the strong support of labor, but thereafter he could never again count on the support of the unions—who supported F.D.R.'s attempt—and many of them opposed him for his renomination in 1946.

By 1940 Wheeler had become one of the greatest crowd pleasers on the isolationist circuit. His appearance at an America First rally was a sure guarantee of a packed house. The fever to keep America out of another war was strong enough to cross party lines and bring together such divergent forces as Socialist Norman Thomas, Republicans Senator Nye and Congressman Fish, as well as Democrat Wheeler and many others besides. However, when war with the Axis finally broke out on December 7, 1941, Wheeler supported all of F.D.R.'s wartime measures.

In the spring of 1940 Wheeler announced that he would be available for the nomination at the Democratic Convention that summer even if F.D.R. decided to seek a third term. He declared that only a noninterventionalist candidate could win in November. John L. Lewis threw his support behind him, but by the time the delegates met Wheeler was out of the running.

Wheeler was the co-author with the late Sam Rayburn of the Utility Holding Company Bill, which he handled in the Senate. The law, subsequently known as the Wheeler-Rayburn Act, was aimed at destroying holding companies that could not clearly prove the economic necessity for their existence.

Throughout his career he stormed against the trusts, including the mining interests and oil companies; he urged rigid regulation of big business. Flouting party leadership, he often sided with Senators Borah of Idaho and Norris of Nebraska, yet in 1933, when he became chairman of the Committee on Interstate Commerce, he served as front man for the Roosevelt Crusade.

During the Democratic Convention of 1944, as well as the previous one in 1940, many political observers chose Wheeler as the man, who, as a vice-presidential candidate, could bring harmony to the party. Many of Roosevelt's closest advisers, pleaded with Wheeler, as they also did in 1940, to run for the vice-presidency. Wheeler refused, and at the conventions it was Wallace and Truman respectively who were chosen.

When Wheeler stood for reelection in 1946 he was defeated. He tells it this way: "In 1946 money was sent in from New York, Hollywood, and other places to defeat me, and some of the labor and farm leaders whom I had befriended when they had few friends were the ones that beat me in the primary. However, that is life, and I have no regrets. As a matter of fact, they did me a favor from the financial standpoint and probably from a health standpoint."

Wheeler has been practicing law since 1947 in partnership with his son in Washington, D.C., with most of their work taking them before the Federal Communications Commission and the Interstate Commerce Commission. Of current events he says: "If I were in the Senate today, I would be supporting some things that the Administration wants and opposing others. I was always an independent in politics and still am. I have always felt we had no business in Vietnam, and that we can't tell every country what kind of government they are going to have. Nor can we buy the friendship of countries any more than you can buy the lasting friendship of individuals."

In his Washington, D.C., law office recently.
George Lohr

Addressing an isolationist rally in 1939.

In 1938.

GALE SONDERGAARD

Gale Sondergaard was a successful stage actress before she entered motion pictures. After studying under Jessie Bonstelle as a member of the famous Bonstelle Players, she appeared on Broadway in a number of plays. Her most important role was that of Nina, in Eugene O'Neill's *Strange Interlude*. In the original 1928 New York company the role was essayed by Lynn Fontanne, who was replaced by Judith Anderson, followed by Miss Sondergaard. That Miss Sondergaard was given so meaty a part already played by two of the most famous actresses in the American theatre is a testimony to the faith the producers had in the young actress.

In the early thirties her husband, Herbert Biberman, a successful stage director in New York for the Theatre Guild, went to Hollywood with a contract to direct pictures. At the time the Bibermans moved to California, Gale decided to give up her career—she had little interest in movies, and felt they were not the proper medium for her.

After Gale settled down in her new home and became used to a life away from Broadway, an agent asked her permission to submit her name for the role of Faith in the classic *Anthony Adverse*. Mervyn LeRoy, who was directing it at Warner Brothers and looking for a face that was unknown to movie audiences, chose her for the part. It was with little enthusiasm that the actress accepted it, though. Even when with an ecstatic LeRoy she saw the rushes she was unimpressed. The role seemed small after what she had become used to on Broadway, and her acting seemed to her to be "self-conscious."

The picture was released in 1936, the year that the Academy of Motion Picture Arts and Sciences added the category of Best Supporting Actress. Gale Sondergaard received the Oscar for her first screen role.

Although her debut role and many others she played were sympathetic ones, Gale Sondergaard is remembered as the Queen of the Heavies. She laughs today when fans refer to her as the Lady They Loved to Hate, and seem to have forgotten that she was Mme. Dreyfus in *The Life of Émile Zola* (1937) and was a foil for Bob Hope and Bing Crosby in *The Road to Rio* (1947). She was, however, a menace in many a movie in the thirties and for-.ties—she played the Eurasian wife of Bette Davis' lover in *The Letter* (murdering Bette in the last reel), Jimmy Stewart threatened to drop her down a manhole after she frightened Simone Simon in *Seventh Heaven,* and she was burned up in a forest after scaring little Shirley Temple in *The Bluebird.*

In 1946 she was once again nominated for the Best Supporting Actress of that year for her performance in *Anna and the King of Siam.* (The picture in which she played the role of Rex Harrison's wife has not been shown on TV because of the musical remake, *The King and I.*)

In 1948 Gale Sondergaard, along with 300 others in Hollywood, was black-listed from the motion picture industry following the famous House Un-American Activities Committee's investigation of the film industry. Her husband was a member of the group, now referred to as "The Hollywood 10," who refused to give testimony to H.U.A.C. and were sent to prison.

Since 1948 Miss Sondergaard has not made a film, television, or radio appearance as an actress though she and Herbert Biberman have been on countless panels and interview shows concerning the blacklist. Professionally, however, they are *personae non gratae* in the entertainment industry.

The Bibermans sold their home in the Hollywood Hills in 1965 and moved to New York City where Gale did an off-Broadway one-woman show in 1966 entitled *Woman.* In it she read works such as *The Doll's House,* concerning the emergence of woman as an independent being.

There is no apparent bitterness in Gale today. She talks easily with young fans who recognize her on the street from her old pictures now playing on *The Late Show* on TV, and exhibits a dazzling smile that belies the troubles she has known. While performing in *Woman* in 1966, her daughter died unexpectedly.

About her career she says, "Yes, I miss acting. A part of my life—a part of me, really—stopped when my work was taken away from me. I miss it every day. I miss it very much indeed."

Today, with husband,
Herbert Biberman.
Edward Oleksak

In a costume by Adrian, circa 1923.

LEATRICE JOY

Leatrice Joy is her real name which seems quite fitting since everything about her is genuine. Her first name was that of her father's old girl friend, her mother had a unique way of teasing him. Joy was her mother's maiden name and predicted the pleasure she would give for so many years to her fans.

Although her career in pictures dates back to 1915, it was not until the early twenties that she became a big star. In the meantime she played an extra in one of Mary Pickford's early movies and was the love interest of both Billy West and Oliver Hardy in the slapstick comedies the two comics made after the First World War.

It was Cecil B. de Mille who made Miss Joy into one of the biggest stars of the silent era. For him she made *Manslaughter* (1922), and the original *Ten Commandments* (1923). The two worked so well together that when de Mille left Paramount to become an independent producer he took Leatrice with him. Leatrice headed an all-star cast for *Java Head* in 1923 and in 1924 she costarred in *Triumph* with Rod La Rocque, who is married to Vilma Banky and lives on their ranch in California.

When she bought a Rolls Royce in 1926 Conrad Nagel told her he thought it was extravagant. "What, darling, does 'extravagance' mean when you are making thousands of dollars a week?" she answered.

Leatrice was neither a vamp nor a sweet young thing. In most of her pictures she was the severely tailored career woman. Much of the popularity of bobbed hair during that period was due to her mannish coiffures.

148

Miss Joy went into semi-retirement in the thirties, living in Beverly Hills, appearing occasionally in a small film part. At that time she fostered the career of one of the best remembered Negro character actresses, Louise Beavers, who was for 12 years Miss Joy's personal maid before peeling grapes for Mae West.

In 1954 Leatrice had a supporting role in a picture called *Love Nest*. Another in the cast was a comedian who had not been too successful. His name was Jack Paar. The ingenue was played by a blonde whom Miss Joy noticed at once in spite of her small part. "She had the bearing of a real star and was gifted with that wonderfully innocent sex appeal that is so rare." Her name was Marilyn Monroe.

Born in New Orleans, there is more than a trace of a Southern drawl in her speech. The farther back into the past she goes the heavier it gets: "I'm never lonely on cold, snowy nights. I have the delightful memories of a wonderful, happy childhood, and a terribly romantic youth. Did you know that John and I eloped to Mexico? A *mariachi* band played "Alexander's Ragtime Band" as our wedding march. Still, it was romantic. Everything was then."

She is still addressed as "Mrs. John Gilbert," although she and the matinee idol were divorced long before he died in 1936. Their grandson is an eleven-year-old aspiring actor, whose agent is also a Paramount star of the silent period, Esther Ralston.

Miss Joy lives in a charming house in Riverside, Connecticut. It is right on the water and is appropriately called "The Magic Cottage." Much of the time its owner is away keeping speaking engagements at women's clubs or visiting friends in Hollywood.

Today: grandmother, lecturer, writer. *John Virzi*

LARRY ADLER

Larry Adler won a contest three weeks after he began playing the mouth organ (he never calls it a "harmonica"), at the age of fourteen. The place was Baltimore, where he was born and grew up. The year was 1928.

His mother encouraged him to "be somebody" which, for a musician, meant go to New York. In the big city he auditioned for the famous Borrah Minnevitch (of "Harmonica Rascal" fame) who told him, "Kid, you stink." Eddie Cantor, Gus Edwards, and Flo Ziegfeld thought otherwise and encouraged him to stick around until he got a break. Each was to say after Adler had made it that he had found the kid playing on the sidewalk for pennies.

Adler didn't have long to wait. By 1934 he was playing the Palace Theatre on Broadway and appearing as a guest on the radio variety shows of the day.

The elevation of Larry Adler to stardom made the harmonica respectable for the first time. Until then the instrument had been reserved for hillbilly acts and blackface performers. Kids began taking it up around the country during the Depression.

In 1935 Adler made his first trip to England. He played in the big musical success of the season, *Streamline*. In 1937 Jack Warner heard him play during an engagement at a Hollywood nightclub, and signed him up for the movie *The Singing Marine*. The director, Busby Berkeley, had no knowledge of the contract until Larry appeared ready for work. Once he heard Adler play he was delighted to change a few of the old scenes around and make what turned out to be the opening, and highlight, of the picture —the harmonicist playing for a group of Marines, including Dick Powell, around a campfire.

By the late thirties Adler was known all over the world through his recordings and movies. In 1939 he played his first symphony concert in Sydney, Australia.

The music he created, which turned the mouth organ into a sophisticated instrument, was appreciated as much by fellow musicians as by the general public. When he played the "Bolero" for its composer, Maurice Ravel listened intently and then told Larry all of the mistakes he had noticed during the piece. Heartsick, Adler asked if Ravel would at least sign the arrangement that Adler had done. "But," said Ravel, "I thought you would allow me to keep it as a souvenir!"

Composers have written works especially for Adler to play. The late Ralph Vaughan Williams and Darius Milhaud, both avid Adler fans, contributed original works to his repertoire, as did Arthur Benjamin and Cyril Scott. Only recently Ira Gershwin gave him an unpublished concerto of the late George Gershwin along with permission to perform it.

As the postwar Red scare began in 1947 Larry Adler along with his longtime friend and frequent partner in recitals, dancer Paul Draper, were accused of being Communists. On advice of attorneys and friends they sued the woman who had brought the charges for libel. The long and costly case ended in a hung jury.

From that day on Larry Adler's services, once sought after by producers in all media, were unwanted. In 1948 Adler, his wife, and three children moved to England where they have lived ever since.

Whatever his political leanings or feelings about his native land, Larry Adler entertained United Nations troops in the front lines during the Korean War in 1952.

Adler has never ceased working in England, and enjoys enormous popularity there. His concerts, benefits, TV appearances, and tours have made him as much of a drawing card there as he ever was in this country. In 1966 his appearance at the Edinburgh Festival was the highlight of the affair.

Although he still comes to the United States for a club or a concert date from time to time, his bookings are in small clubs rather than the places that used to carry his name proudly on a marquee. Neither the TV networks nor the motion picture studios seem interested in his abilities. Although he has done the musical scores for major motion pictures such as *The Great Chase* (1965) and *King and Country* (1966), it was usually under another name to protect the studios. The notable exception was the English film *Genevieve* which starred the late Kay Kendall, and received an Academy Award nomination in 1954 for the Best Original Musical Score.

Adler says of his adopted country: "England has a sense of tolerance and fair play I hope some day will be present in the United States. My friend Paul has recently moved back to New York. He tells me things have changed. I'm afraid they will have to change a good deal more than they have before I return."

At the height of his fame, 1945, just two years before he was blacklisted, and (*right*) during a recent visit to New York.

NBC Radio   *William Glenesk*

JOHN W. BRICKER

Senator John W. Bricker was born in 1893 and grew up on a farm in Mount Sterling, Ohio. He earned a law degree at Ohio State University. After serving as a First Lieutenant in World War I, he went into law practice in 1920 in Columbus, Ohio, becoming Assistant Attorney General in 1923 and Attorney General in 1933.

In 1939 Bricker was elected Governor of Ohio on the Republican ticket serving a total of three terms. His terms in office were marked by fiscal responsibility and a determination to check the expanding power of the federal government. Bricker went so far as to resist appeals by Ohio cities for emergency relief from Washington.

At the G.O.P. national convention in 1940 it was Governor Bricker who urged that the nomination of Wendell Willkie be made unanimous, following an exhausting and bitter fight between the Old Guard and the internationalists in the Republican party. When Bricker asked that all Republicans join in the cry "We Want Willkie," it was a plea for party unity and a dramatic national debut by the man who had his eye on the nomination four years thence.

The Conservative wing of the G.O.P. had been foiled in its attempt to nominate one of their own in 1936 and in 1940. In 1944, although General MacArthur's name received more than passing mention, among the professionals it was John Bricker of Ohio who was the leading contender from the Right—the war was still being fought, and MacArthur was in the Pacific. Bricker, on the other hand, was very much available for press conferences and speeches, and he controlled the powerful Ohio delegation. He had the added benefit of being endorsed by one of the most influential and skillful politicians in his party, Senator Robert A. Taft, also of Ohio. Bricker announced his candidacy on November 16, 1943.

Although Bricker was unable to capture the Presidential nomination, Governor Thomas E. Dewey of New York took on the Ohio governor as running mate. Dewey and Bricker seemed an unlikely combination, even in a profession known for its strange bedfellows—the New York Governor was viewed by the Old Guard as a liberal and an internationalist. The Dewey-Bricker ticket was defeated by the Roosevelt-Truman team, who campaigned with the seemingly logical slogan "Don't Change Horses in the Middle of a Stream." Presidents had traditionally been reelected during wartime, and the results were no great surprise.

If there is an American public official more easily forgotten than a vice-president it is the man who only ran for the office. Bricker, however, achieved fame far greater than second-in-command would ever have afforded him, merely by proposing one piece of legislation. He had been elected Senator from Ohio in 1946 on principles and promises even more to the Right of fellow Ohioan Senator Taft. He remained a consistent foe of centralized government and this country's growing involvement in international affairs. It was his fear of America's direction in world politics that led him to create the famous Bricker Amendment. The Amendment would make any treaty or agreement with a foreign country invalid if it conflicted with the United States Constitution, and made all treaties and agreements subject to two-thirds approval by the Senate.

Bricker's fear of the infringement on our national sovereignty was shared by the American Medical Association, the Daughters of the American Revolution, and an organization made up of mothers of overseas armed forces personnel known as the Vigilant Mothers for the Bricker Amendment.

Although the Amendment was defeated in the Senate by a vote of 42 to 50 on February 25, 1954, the following day Senator Walter F. George proposed a watered-down version which received the necessary two-thirds majority with a vote of 61 to 30. On the crucial motion to send the amendment to the states for ratification, however, the vote was 60–31, one less than the number needed.

The Bricker Amendment died hard. It was proposed four times in the Senate over the next four sessions. The last time it was up for a vote was 1958. It was defeated as was its author by his Democratic opponent Mike DiSalle in the senatorial elections of 1958.

No one, least of all Bricker, expected he would lose that election. He returned to law practice with his old firm of Bricker, Evatt, Barton, Eckler and Neihoff in Columbus, Ohio. One of the partners in the firm is John Day Bricker, his only son. In 1964 rumors were about in Ohio politics that Bricker would oppose Senator Stephen Young in the senate race of that year, but he chose otherwise. His continued interest in politics precludes office-holding. He refuses to say whom he would like to see as the upcoming G.O.P. presidential nominee, but when George Romney first ran for the governorship in Michigan former Senator Bricker referred to a Senate hearing years ago when Romney, then an auto executive, was queried by Bricker: "One of the most able witnesses I've ever seen," said Bricker of his witness, "an excellent choice for anything he wants." (In 1964 Bricker was solidly behind Senator Barry Goldwater.)

John W. Bricker is on the Board of Trustees of Ohio State University and Franklin College. He is a 33-degree Shriner and is active in the American Legion.

With Mrs. John W. Bricker on the campaign trail in 1944, and (*right*) during a recent visit.

Jacob Lofman

With Ann Dvorak in the popular 1932 flick *Crooner*.

DAVID MANNERS

Before leaving his home in Halifax, Nova Scotia, where he was born in 1901, Rauff Acklom changed his name to David Manners. In New York the future Hollywood leading man studied drama and worked with the Theatre Guild.

When Manners arrived in Hollywood in 1929 he was exactly what the studios were looking for. The new sound systems had ended the career of many silent stars, and the casting offices were told to find actors who could speak properly. David's stage training had provided him with the proper diction, and nature had given him the clean-cut good looks that fit so many parts being cast at the time. His first picture, and probably his best part, was in the classic *Journey's End* (1930) from the enormously successful stage play. A contract with First National Pictures resulted from that picture.

Manners was aptly named. His first name might have been "Good" considering his image at the time. Always well dressed, well spoken, and with impeccable manners, David was a perfect leading man for aspiring young actresses and older female stars who wanted nobody stealing scenes from them with mannerisms or too much sex appeal. This young man was just right and every actress wanted him in her picture. He was what girls in those days called "a good catch,"playing an earnest, sincere young man with the kind of good looks that needn't worry parents unduly. David wasn't the type of fellow to let the public down—he was always the perfect gentleman with Loretta Young, Mae Clarke (who won a tidy settlement from a Los Angeles TV station a few years ago when an old woman who emceed a horror movie claimed to be she), Joan Blondell, and Ann Dvorak.

154

It is unfortunate that Manners, who made so many pictures in the thirties, was in so few that really hold up by today's standards. The only two which are shown today at art houses as cinema classics are *Journey's End* (1930) and Katharine Hepburn's first film, *A Bill of Divorcement* (1932). Although he never played a "heavy," he is associated with horror films because of his appearance in *Dracula* (1931), the original sound version, *The Mummy* (1932), in which his leading lady was Zita Johann, now living in West Nyack, New York, and *The Black Cat* (1934).

While his career in films didn't last beyond the late thirties his credit list is a long one. A few of the better pictures were: the first sound version of *Kismet* (1930) with Otis Skinner, *The Millionaire* (1931) opposite Evelyn Knapp (now Mrs. Snyder of Beverly Hills, California), *Man Wanted* (1932) with Kay Francis (next to Greta Garbo, no star has drawn a tighter curtain around her life since her retirement in the late forties. Living just off Fifth Avenue in New York's East sixties, Miss Francis refuses to sign autographs, to be photographed, or interviewed), *Crooner* (1932), *The Greeks Had a Word for It* (1932) with Ina Claire (completely retired to a very social life in San Francisco, California), and *Mystery of Edwin Drood* (1935) with Heather Angel (now Mrs. Robert B. Sinclair of Montecito, California). David also made several pictures with the lovely European star Elissa Landi (who died of cancer in 1948), *Warrior's Husband* (1933), and *The Great Flirtation* (1934), after which he lived in relative obscurity.

In 1946 he attempted a comeback on Broadway in the production *Truckline Café* but the play was not successful. Also in the cast was a young actor, Marlon Brando.

During the fifties David turned to writing. Since then he has completed three novels under the name David J. Manners. He is currently working on his fourth book.

Manners, who has never married, lives in a beautiful home in Pacific Palisades, California, where he enjoys being a Sunday painter and gardener.

Now a successful novelist.

John Virzi

During one of his first interviews after being appointed to Hiram Johnson's Senate seat in 1945.
CBS

WILLIAM F. KNOWLAND

Senator William Fife Knowland was born in 1908 in Alameda, California, the son of the owner-publisher of the Oakland *Tribune*. He attended the University of California, graduating in 1926.

After college he worked on his father's paper. He became a California State Assemblyman, serving from 1933 until 1935, and a state Senator serving from 1935 until 1939.

During the Second World War he was a commissioned officer with the United States Army. Upon his discharge Knowland was appointed by California Governor Earl Warren, an old political crony, to serve the remaining year of the term of Hiram W. Johnson, who had died. Knowland was elected to a full term on his own in 1946.

Knowland was one of the youngest and brashest senators on Capitol Hill. Usually the Senate deals with such behavior as his by ignoring the upstart, but Bill Knowland had an integrity and energy that won him friends among his colleagues and a good reputation with the press. He was reelected in 1952, and a year later, in spite of his lack of seniority, became majority leader. He served in that capacity during Eisenhower's first two years in office and thereafter as minority leader until 1957.

One of the surest signs in American politics that an officeholder has Presidential fever is when he makes a concerted effort to appear both liberal and conservative at the same time. "Middle-of-the-road" was the popular expression during the Eisenhower era, and Knowland did his utmost to seem right on the double line. He was a diligent worker on behalf of Ike's domestic programs, or at least most of them. It was in the field of foreign affairs that his natural instincts toward the Right betrayed themselves. Knowland fought hard for the Bricker Amendment, and even after it seemed dead and buried could be counted on to say a few good words about it. The China lobby in Washington had no stronger ally than the senior Senator from California. His stands for a blockade of the Chinese mainland and against the admission of the People's Republic of China to the United

Nations were so vehement and so often repeated that they earned him the title of "the Senator from Formosa."

When in 1957 *Time* magazine did its cover story on Knowland, Joe McCarthy's power was over, and he was only a few months away from his death (Knowland had voted against the censure of Senator McCarthy), Robert Taft had been gone for several years, and Eisenhower was in his second and final term as President. The final assessment of Knowland's potential then was that next to Richard Nixon he was the most powerful man in his party. In a way his position was more advantageous than the Vice-President's since he could be freer in his public utterances. However, as a political thinker, he was dismissed as a "young fogy."

Exactly what Knowland had in mind when he quit the Senate in 1958 to run for the governorship of California may never be known. It was then nearly a foregone conclusion that Vice-President Nixon would have the G.O.P. Presidential nomination sewed up in 1960. Knowland might have figured Nixon for a loser and, perhaps, intended to sit it out for six years and take the nomination in 1964. One thing is certain, he definitely had his eye on the White House.

The Republican governor of the Golden State at the time was Goodwin Knight, also no pal of Nixon's. Knowland and Nixon pressured Knight into running for the Senate, much against his will. Knowland then proceeded to run on a platform that included "right-to-work" laws. Both he and Knight went down to humiliating defeat at the polls. It was a beating that all but wrecked the California G.O.P. (When Nixon tried for the same post in 1962 Knight gave him nearly as much trouble in the primaries as the Democrats did in the general election.)

Knowland never again tried for public office, although just about every time a California election approaches his name is mentioned for one office or another. He took over the Oakland *Tribune* after his father retired a few years ago, and he and the paper have remained loyal to the G.O.P., with Knowland being a willing campaigner for candidates in areas where he is still popular around the state. The former Senator is a pilot and belongs to a club of civilians who have broken the sound barrier. He lives in Piedmont with his wife. They have three children.

At a recent press conference on California politics in San Francisco. *UPI*

FRED A. HARTLEY

The man who successfully coauthored one of the most controversial pieces of legislation in the last forty years, the Taft-Hartley Act, was born in Harrison, New Jersey, in 1902. Fred A. Hartley was graduated from Rutgers University, and held various municipal offices in Kearney, New Jersey, including that of Police and Fire Commissioner before he was elected to the House of Representatives in 1929.

In his first Congressional election it looked for awhile as though he had been defeated by his Democratic opponent, but after a recount Hartley was adjudged the winner. He entered the House at the age of twenty-six, just one year over the minimum required, the youngest Congressman in that session.

Hartley admits to having entered politics as a liberal, but by the thirties he had become an isolationist and voted against lend-lease and the revision of the Neutrality Act. For the first 14 years of his tenure in office he had the support of the A.F.L., which was no small consideration to a Congressman who represented an area nearly completely industrial.

Some of the legislation that Hartley was responsible for during his ten consecutive terms in office was a physical fitness bill, the franking privilege to servicemen overseas during World War II, and the extra ration of gas allotted to civilians for vacations during World War II. Like many of the isolationists the tag of "anti-Semite" was one he had to avoid at every corner. In the 1930's, after he proposed his bill to promote physical fitness, someone compared his proposals to those of Hitler. Hartley was quick to point out that the cosponsor of the bill was a New York legislator, Sammy Weiss.

During the war Hartley voted for strike control bills and opposed "portal-to-portal pay," a main objective of unions at the time. Although he had supported such legislation as a pro-A.F.L. amendment to the Wagner Labor Act during the thirties, by the end of World War II he and the unions had parted political company.

When the 80th Congress was elected overwhelmingly Republican, Hartley said: "The mandate of this Congress was to protect the public from violence, loss of output and class hatred due to increasing labor disputes, to protect the workers from political and financial exploitation by union leaders, and to save the American system of free opportunity and free enterprise." By this time he was admittedly right of Senator Robert A. Taft of Ohio.

In 1947 with postwar strikes rampant in the United States, Hartley was the youngest chairman of any Congressional committee, heading the powerful House Education and Labor Committee. The official title of the bill he wrote with Robert Taft was the Labor Management Act of 1947. It passed both chambers in early June only to be vetoed by President Truman. It is Hartley's opinion that Truman acted under political pressure by the unions rather than from conviction. On June 23 the veto was overridden, and on August 22, 1947, the Taft-Hartley Act became the law of the land.

Hartley maintains to this day that the law benefits labor unions as well as employers, and that such was his intent when he wrote it. Bridling at the suggestion that he is antilabor he indignantly points out that he is and has been a union member all of his adult life.

Supporters of the bill called it the "worker's bill of rights." *The New York Times* editorialized: "It is an attempt . . . to see to it that organized labor does not trespass as it has been doing so flagrantly upon rights of management, the individual worker and the general public."

Fred Hartley chose not to seek reelection in 1948. His district had been gerrymandered, and he was then living in another area of New Jersey. The vendetta that the unions had threatened played no small part in his decision.

Although he retired from politics, Hartley kept an office in Washington, and acted as a business consultant there and in New Jersey until 1961 when he suffered a stroke which paralyzed one side of his body. Hartley had, however, been a fine athlete during his Rutgers days, and never allowed himself to get out of condition. He responded to treatment, and by 1965 was driving his Mercedes Benz around the New Jersey countryside near his farm in Milford. He lives quietly in a large ultramodern ranch home with his wife and several Great Danes.

About Republicanism today Hartley says, "Taft was ahead of his time. He warned the G.O.P. that it would have to take the initiative in proposing social legislation. Personally, I am opposed to the [Liberal Republicanism] turn the party has taken but as a practical politician I can see that it has to be done."

The Congressman in his office, 1936.
Harris & Ewing

In retirement now.

Wishing all her fans a Merry
Christmas in 1929.

PATSY RUTH MILLER

The silent screen star was born in St. Louis, Missouri, in 1905. She was
educated at various Roman Catholic schools before her father, a drama
critic for a local newspaper, moved the family to Los Angeles when she
was in her early teens.

Patsy has appeared in films since 1920, including a small part in *Camille*
(1921) with Rudolph Valentino and Alla Nazimova, and in *Omar the Tent-
maker* (1922). The picture that made her a star, however, was the original
Lon Chaney silent version of *The Hunchback of Notre Dame* (1923)—she
portrayed the dancing girl, Esmerelda, the role that was to overshadow
everything she did after that.

Some of her credits during the silent era after becoming a star are: *Why
Girls Go Back Home* (1926), *The White Black Sheep* (1926) with Richard
Barthelmess, *Private Izzy Murphy* (1926), *Oh, What a Nurse* (1926), *Broken
Hearts of Hollywood* (1926), *What Every Girl Should Know* (1926), *Hell
Bent for Heaven* (1926), *Wolf's Clothing* (1927), *Hot Heels* (1928), *Beauti-
ful but Dumb* (1928), *Red Riders of Canada* (1928), and *No Gate Crasher*
(1928).

While turning out such pictures, Patsy was living in the style expected
of silent stars. She drove a Pierce-Arrow and gave her kid brother Winston
a Stutz Bearcat which she bought from Constance Talmadge. (Winston
Miller is now a producer-writer at his sister's old lot, Universal, which has
passed through several hands since the days of its first czar, Carl Laemmle.
Carl, Jr., son of the founder and also a producer during Patsy's era, lives
quietly in Manhattan.)

Her talkies include the all-star *Show of Shows* (1929) in which Patsy was
one of the Floradora Girls, *Night Beat* (1931), and her last, *Lonely Wives*
(1931) with Edward Everett Horton and Laura La Plante (a close friend

of Miss Miller's over the years, married to screen producer Irving Asher and living in an ultramodern house in Palm Desert.)

After Patsy's career in talkies failed to materialize she began to write. Throughout the thirties and forties she wrote radio scripts and magazine stories that were published in *The New Yorker* and other top publications. In 1934 and 1936 her short stories received honorable mention at the O. Henry Awards. She also wrote a novel, in 1939, called *That Flanagan Girl. By* the time she decided to give it all up Patsy had a considerable following for her work among mystery story fans.

The former star married the prominent New York importer, E. S. Deans whom she met in 1951 while on vacation in the Bahamas. They live in an enormous house with frontage on Long Island Sound in Stamford, Connecticut. Much of their time is spent traveling—Patsy has been around the world several times and at least once a year gets to Hollywood for a visit with some of her contemporaries like Helen Ferguson (now Mrs. Hargrave of Beverly Hills).

One of Patsy's neighbors and close friend is the silent star, Jacqueline Logan, now a pillar of the John Birch Society in Bedford Hills, New York. They are active in local politics together, Patsy describing herself as "a conservative Republican." She says "I was for Goldwater in 1964 and for Taft before that. You can put me down as a 100 percent constitutionalist."

Patsy is asked constantly about Valentino. At the time she made her film with him he had not yet become a household name. To the question what was he really like she replies, "Rudy was everything he wasn't on the screen. He was refined and courteous. I deeply resent some of the things I have seen written about him recently. The fact is that he was from an excellent Italian family and was a perfect gentleman and a wonderful friend to all of us who knew him."

Of the past Miss Miller concludes, "I seldom think about it, but I am grateful for having been associated with the movie industry at a time at which, I believe, it was at its peak. I guess I'm not good copy. I liked all of the people I worked with, but I haven't time to miss any of it. My life now is everything I could possibly ask for."

Today too busy for most things except traveling.

John Virzi

Jenkins during the hearings, 1954.

RAY H. JENKINS

In 1954 Ray H. Jenkins, a criminal lawyer practicing in Knoxville, Tennessee, was picked by the Senate Subcommittee on Congressional Investigations to represent that body in the famous Army-McCarthy hearings. Several months later he was the most famous attorney in the United States.

Jenkins was suggested to the Committee by Senator Everett Dirksen, whom he had met previously in another connection, and went to Washington for what he recalls as, "a more merciless, searching, cruel cross-examination that I had ever inflicted upon the most bloodthirsty murderer whom I had prosecuted in Court. They were a wily, foxy group of men. I didn't know at the time, but from time to time one would slip out of the room, and it developed that he was talking long-distance to people in Tennessee whose names I had dropped, including the members of our Supreme Court, the Court of Appeals, the trial courts, the editors of the Knoxville newspapers, lawyers, and public officials."

While Senators Mundt, Jackson, Symington, McClellan, Dworshak, and Potter were interviewing Jenkins, the F.B.I. was making a thorough check on his personal life. "Finally," says Jenkins, "when they had me hanging on the ropes, I was excused from the room, and a caucus was held. Senator Mundt called me back and smilingly said, 'Ray, you're it.'"

The battle between Secretary of the Army Stevens and Senator McCarthy had been widely publicized. The honor and integrity of both had been brought into question. The hearings, nationally televised for all to see and hear, started out to be an orderly dignified procedure but soon degenerated into a brawl, and orderliness surrendered to pandemonium. What should have been concluded within a few weeks went on and on interminably for the better part of two months.

A thick-necked, gravel-voiced man, Jenkins bent over backwards to be impartial during the stormy hearings. He was rewarded for his efforts by being accused by both sides of favoritism.

After the great battle Jenkins returned to Knoxville, and is there today still practicing criminal law. The 25,000 letters and wires he received during and after the hearings are still in storage—he has never opened one of them. Jenkins on the verdict in retrospect: "These seven dedicated senators wrote a report in effect finding both parties guilty as charged. It was a correct verdict. It reflected the consensus of opinion of the American people." And on Senator McCarthy: "I feel history will evaluate Senator McCarthy as a blustering, dynamic but reckless individual, devoid of any feeling of the consequences of the rashness in his utterances. At the same time, however, he, more than any man of his generation, alerted the nation to the one great overriding issue in the world, and to its danger—communism.

"Had Senator McCarthy been able to control his tongue, his temper, and his intemperance he might have become the President of the United States."

Today, the Army-McCarthy hearings a distant roar. *Skeet Talent Studio*

In his famous straw boater, with cane, 1931. *Maurice Seymour*

HARRY RICHMAN

The musical star, born in 1895 in Cincinnati, Ohio, was doing a vaudeville single in blackface at the age of twelve. As a teenager he was part of a team called Remington and Richman, interrupting his show business career during the First World War to serve in the United States Navy.

In the early twenties he was the accompanist both for Mae West and the Dolly Sisters (Jenny is dead and Rozicka divides her time between New York City and Palm Springs), and at the time roomed with Bugs Baer and Damon Runyon.

After appearances in *Varieties of 1922, Queen of Hearts* (1923), opposite the late Nora Bayes, and the *George White Scandals of 1926* Richman had become a big enough name to have his own speakeasy, "Club Richman" on Park Avenue.

Some of his other Broadway shows were: *Sons o' Guns* (1929) with Lily Damita (who lives most of the time in Palm Beach, Florida), *Ziegfeld Follies* (1931), *George White Music Hall Varieties* (1932), *International Review* (1933), and *Say When* (1934) with Bob Hope. His last Broadway show was *New Priorities of 1943*.

On the movie side, Richman starred in one of the earliest and most successful film musicals, *Puttin' on the Ritz* (1930), with Aileen Pringle. His other pictures were *Music Goes Round* (1936), *Stars Over Arizona* (1937), and *Kicking the Moon Around* (1938), which he made in England.

Richman figured in one of the first of the famous radio "feuds," which was broadcast in 1927 from his nightly floor show in New York. He and Nils T. Granlund engaged in a series of running arguments done for laughs and publicity. They got both, and started a trend in the new media that produced the famous Ben Bernie-Walter Winchell, and Jack Benny-Fred Allen feuds.

At the height of their careers in the late twenties he and Clara Bow made headlines with their on-again off-again romance. His popularity was just as great in England where he packed the Palladium and Café de Paris during several visits in the thirties.

During his engagements at the Palace Theatre he introduced two new-comers—Kate Smith and Lillian Roth.

Richman collaborated on a number of songs and introduced many others which are associated with him, such as "Laugh, Clown, Laugh" and "Put-tin' on the Ritz." Three standards he wrote are "There's Danger in Your Eyes, Chérie," "Singing a Vagabond Song," both in 1930, and "Walking My Baby Back Home" in 1931.

During the forties he was a guest on every top radio show, singing and clowning with his friends Eddie Cantor, Ben Bernie, George Jessel, and Rudy Vallee. He was on many occasions the headliner in 1944, 1945, and 1946 at the Roxy, Paramount, and Capitol theatres in New York City.

After being out of the spotlight for several years Richman had a minor success in 1959 when he appeared in Miami and Las Vegas in a nightclub review, *Newcomers of 1926–68*. In 1963 he played the Desert Inn in Las Vegas and the Latin Quarter in New York as a single.

Harry Richman was married to model Yvonne Epstein, to former Zieg-feld girl Hazel Froidebaux, and to dancer Yvonne Day. He has been single since 1954.

He has been living frugally in semi-retirement in North Hollywood, California. Since the late forties when he became inactive in show business he has been spending his time visiting friends and writing his life story, recently published as *A Hell of a Life,* in collaboration with Richard Geh-man. He is in excellent health, has the companionship of a pet squirrel, and rehearses constantly, but with no intention of resuming work on a regular schedule.

Enjoying retirement in
Southern California.
Clifford May

With Victor McLaglen in *Professional Soldier* (1936).

FREDDIE BARTHOLOMEW

Born in Ireland in 1924 and brought up in Wilshire, England, by his grandparents and aunt, the future child star was spotted by a studio talent scout while on a holiday in New York City. At the age of ten he was chosen for the title role in the motion picture classic *David Copperfield* (1934), in which he costarred with W. C. Fields.

Thereafter he appeared in such movies as *Anna Karenina* (1935) with Greta Garbo as the mother who walks out of his life, *The Devil Is a Sissy* (1936) with Jackie Cooper, *Captains Courageous* (1937), in which he braved torrential storms with Spencer Tracy, *Kidnapped* (1938) with Warner Baxter, *Lord Jeff* (1938) with Mickey Rooney, and *Swiss Family Robinson* (1940), making the best of a shipwreck.

Through it all he maintained such composure and good manners that he became one of the biggest box office draws throughout the entire period. But to any boy who grew up during that era Freddie will always be the personification of the sissy that he played in *Little Lord Fauntleroy* (1936).

Freddie's private life was nearly as fraught with troubles as his screen roles. In 1937 his aunt, who had raised him and was his legal guardian, was unsuccessfully challenged in the courts by his mother and father who wanted their son back once he had become one of MGM's most valuable properties. Freddie testified that he loved only "Aunt Sissy," and hardly knew his parents. That same year Millicent Bartholomew, "Aunt Sissy," appeared with Freddie again in court in an attempt to have him released from his MGM contract. The terms of the contract, which as his legal guardian she had approved at the time, guaranteed the boy $700 weekly to begin with and would be raised to $1,000 weekly by the end of a seven-year period. Since Freddie was the hottest male child actor in Hollywood at the time his aunt deemed the salary insufficient. The court ruled against her.

Freddie made no movies of any consequence after 1940. (His appearance in *Yank at Eaton* in 1942 was well received but it was Mickey Rooney's picture.) After making millions for Hollywood studios he was reduced to making B pictures such as *Naval Academy* (1941) and *The Town Went Wild* (1944) both with Jimmy Lydon (now a producer at Warner Brothers), the boy who made a career out of playing "Henry Aldrich." His roles became smaller and smaller, and the movies got worse.

During World War II he joined the Air Corps and became a United States citizen. After his discharge he toured the country on the strawhat circuit, having a minor success in the late forties and in 1947 he appeared in *Sepia Cinderella*, a Billy Daniels starrer for RKO.

In 1949 Freddie accepted a job with the New York TV station WPIX as host of an afternoon movie program. Gradually he began directing shows, and became interested in the production of television commercials. "I was a very good television director, to tell you the truth," says Freddie.

In 1954 he joined the advertising agency of Benton & Bowles, one of the largest in the world, becoming in 1965 a vice-president and assigned to one of their largest accounts.

Bartholomew's job takes him back to Hollywood perhaps a dozen times a year. The studios that used to turn out his pictures are now making the commercials and series his agency considers for purchase. Many of the technicians, however, are the same ones who knew the former actor as a boy star.

He seldom sees any of the actors he used to work with. A former child actress he recently ran into in New York and lunched with was Edith Fellows, now taking college courses in Manhattan while trying to decide whether or not to pursue her acting career. Freddie was recently surprised to learn that another MGM moppet of his era, Tommy Kelly, is the Co-ordinator of Youth Opportunities for the Santa Ana, California, schools.

Fred, as he is now called, commutes daily from his home in nearby New Jersey, where he lives with his second wife, a stepdaughter, and a boy and girl of his own. In the garage is a collection of foreign and domestic sports cars—his hobby.

In his current role at Benton & Bowles, Inc.

John Virzi

ARTHUR TRACY: "The Street Singer"

The famous balladeer was born in Philadelphia, the fifth in a family of seven children. His father was an accountant and Tracy's original goal was to become an architect. Arthur won first prizes for singing in his city and state while studying at the famed Curtis Institute of Music. In the early twenties while preparing to enter a national singing contest, a scout for the Shuberts offered him the lead in a touring company of *Blossom Time*. Traveling about the United States with that production he ran the gamut of show business available to an entertainer during those years: vaudeville, burlesque, legitimate theatre, concerts, and stock companies.

While picking up valuable experience moving around the United States, Arthur also studied the languages of the various nationals pouring into this country after the First World War. Much of his success is attributed to his ability to sing in ten different languages, from Japanese to Yiddish.

Tracy was a personality whose fame was made by radio almost overnight. He was heard on radio in Philadelphia when the medium was still at the cat's whiskers stage in 1923 and 1924. He gave it another try during 1929 and 1930 in New York, beginning for nothing and finally working up to a salary of $95.00 a week. His first sponsor was an exterminating company. In 1931 Bill Paley of CBS put him on three times a week on a six-week trial basis. By the time the fifth week came around it was obvious by the fan mail that the network had a valuable property on its hands and that the Street Singer would have to announce his real name to his fans. Up until that time he had appeared merely by title on radio.

Those were the days of titles. There was "The Songbird of the South" (Kate Smith), "The Idol of the Airlanes" (Jan Garber), and "The Red-Headed Music Maker" (Arthur Godfrey). Tracy named himself "The Street Singer." The title became so famous that many today who remember it have to think a minute before they can recall that it belonged to Arthur Tracy.

One of his early radio programs was Chesterfield's *Music That Satisfies* in 1932 which also featured Ruth Etting and the Boswell Sisters.

Arthur had appeared in Hollywood's *Big Broadcast* (1932), the first of the famous series of all-star movies, after reaching stardom on radio.

During that year Arthur's theme song "Marta" (rambling rose of the wildwood) which had sold records in the millions in the United States became a two million seller in England. Due to his initial success there he became one of the most popular singers in the British Isles, and three years later he responded to the demand and sailed for what was supposed to have been a limited personal appearance tour. Rather than being content with seeing their idol and continuing his popularity, his presence seemed to make him an even greater star. The result was that he stayed until just a few days before the outbreak of World War II. During that period he wrote and appeared in four movies, one with Lilli Palmer, one with Margaret Lockwood, and another with Anna Neagle (who is still active in England in plays and television).

The Street Singer has played the Palace and the Roxy in New York City, the Palladium in London, and given one Command Performance. He has recorded over 600 songs.

Through the forties Arthur resumed his radio shows—sponsored by Ex-Lax—made some movie shorts, and was a headliner at nightclubs in New York, Chicago, Hollywood, and Las Vegas.

In 1950 Tracy began to cut down on his theatrical activities to devote more time to his real estate holdings. He invested in Brentwood Village in Washington, D.C., and Oxford Circle in Philadelphia, and is a very popular landlord among the children of the tenants whom he takes for trips to the zoo or just for a drive in his Cadillac when he visits these cities.

Tracy attributes his success on the air to the training he got during his free and low salary days. He went without meals many times, and bought the station's engineers pints of liquor to curry their friendship and learn just how that strange contraption called a microphone worked—Tracy was a favorite of listeners right from the beginning of his Columbia trial because he had mastered the technique necessary for singing over the air.

His latest appearances were on *The Ed Sullivan Show* in 1963 and at the Concord Hotel in New York's Catskills in 1964.

The street on which Arthur does most of his singing these days is West 57th Street where he lives in a large apartment full of the antiques he collected over the years. When people ask what he is doing he tells them that he is "clipping coupons" but makes no secret that he would like very much to be back in front of an audience and is always among the first to volunteer his services for benefits.

He is presently writing his life story, in which Hollywood studios have already shown interest. The title will be, of course, *The Street Singer*.

Circa 1933, at the height of his popularity.

Today, ready and willing to make a comeback.
Maurice Seymour

In *Theodora Goes Wild* (1936).

IRENE DUNNE

One of the screen's most delightful ladies was born in Louisville, Kentucky, in 1904. She went to school at the Chicago College of Music and in 1920 made her stage debut in that city.

In 1922 New York saw her for the first time, when she appeared in the play *The Clinging Vine* which starred Peggy Wood. The next part she had was in *Lollipop* on Broadway in 1924 and was back the following year in *City Chap*. Then came *Sweetheart Time* in 1926 followed by *Yours Truly* in 1927, which starred Leon Errol. In 1928 she was in two shows: *Luckee Girl,* and *She's My Baby* with Clifton Webb and Beatrice Lillie. In 1929 she toured the United States in the role of Magnolia in Flo Ziegfeld's production of *Showboat*.

Miss Dunne then went to Hollywood. Her first motion picture was *Leathernecking* (1930), followed by *Present Arms* the same year. Her first big picture and the one that made her a star was *Cimarron* (1931), also making that year *Consolation Marriage* with Pat O'Brien. She made *Back Street* (1932), and although filmed twice since, movie buffs insist that the Irene Dunne version is the best, *Silver Cord* (1933) with Joel McCrea and *No Other Woman* (1933) with Charles Bickford, *Age of Innocence* (1934) and *Sweet Adeline* (1935). She starred in the highly successful screen version of *Showboat* (1936) and *Theodora Goes Wild* (1936), with Melvyn Douglas for which she received her first of four Oscar nominations.

When people speak of the wonderful light comedies made during the

170

thirties they are usually referring to the pictures turned out by Carole Lombard, Jean Arthur, and Irene Dunne. The three ladies made airy, sophisticated pieces of foolishness that stand up today remarkably well. In fact Miss Dunne's charm has been an embarrassment to more than one actress in a remake of one of her pictures—invariably critics would compare the new version to the original most unfavorably. (*Magnificent Obsession* in 1954 didn't have the magic Robert Taylor and Irene were able to generate in 1935, and in spite of all the money spent in 1965 on *Cimarron* it was generally agreed that Richard Dix and Miss Dunne won the West more interestingly.)

Unfortunately, some of Irene's best pictures cannot be seen on television or in movie art houses because they were remade as films or done as Broadway musicals and therefore the originals are withheld from distribution, among them *Roberta* (1935) with Fred Astaire and Ginger Rogers, and *Anna and the King of Siam* (1946).

Her other screen credits include: *The Awful Truth* (1937) with Cary Grant, *Love Affair* (1939) with Charles Boyer, *My Favorite Wife* (1940) again with Grant and his roommate at the time, Randolph Scott, *Penny Serenade* (1941) a Dunne-Grant classic tearjerker, *A Guy Named Joe* (1943) with Spencer Tracy, *White Cliffs of Dover* (1944), and from the Broadway stage *Over 21* (1945), *Life With Father* (1947), *I Remember Mama* (1948). Irene played Queen Victoria in *The Mudlark* (1950) but it was unsuccessful at the box office. Her last motion picture was *It Grows on Trees* (1952) and in 1956 she was seen on TV's *Ford Theatre* in a play.

In 1957 she was an Alternate Delegate at the twelfth session of the United Nations General Assembly. Irene always had a keen interest in politics, campaigning for Republican candidates in a number of California races. She is also active in various Catholic charities.

She was married from 1928 to a dentist, Francis Griffin, until his death in 1965. They had one daughter. Irene still lives in her West Los Angeles home. Irene has never announced her retirement, but she has turned down countless offers of movie, stage, and television work over the past decade.

Arriving at a recent opening.
Francis Young

On the crest of her wave of popularity, 1941.

PAULETTE GODDARD

The date of Paulette Goddard's birth has never actually been verified. Most film historians agreed that it was sometime close to 1911. Like Oscar Wilde, Marion Levee (her real name), believes that a woman who would tell her real age would tell anything. What is known about the girl from Great Neck, Long Island, is that she had an uncle named Goddard who was a close friend of the producer Flo Ziegfeld. She prevailed upon Goddard to use his influence with the impressario to get her a job on the stage. When the Great Ziegfeld hired his show girls, talent and experience were not what he looked for as they seldom had anything to do but look gorgeous. He signed the high school girl and put her into *No Foolin'* which was a hit on Broadway in 1926. Paulette played a popular headline personality of the day, "Peaches" Browning, in a skit with another unknown at the time, Claire Luce. (When asked about Paulette recently Miss Luce said, "Even then she had something. There was a vivacity and pertness that you couldn't help but notice.") Paulette became one of Ziegfeld's favorites, and the next year he put her in *Rio Rita*. She met and married her first husband around that time. He was Edward James, president of the Southern States Lumber Company, and for a while she lived with him in Asheville, North Carolina.

By 1931 Paulette had left her husband, driven to Reno for a divorce (in a Dusenberg), and arrived in Hollywood where she landed a contract with Hal Roach at $100 a week. After six months she was let go. She appeared in a few musicals of the period, such as *The Kid From Spain* (1932) with Eddie Cantor. Her parts were tiny, usually no more than a member of the chorus, as she was for Busby Berkeley in one of his extravaganzas.

How and where she and Charlie Chaplin met is as mysterious as nearly everything else about their relationship. In 1934 the comedian announced that he had found the girl he had searched for to essay the role of the waif

172

in his film *Modern Times*. They worked on the picture two years, and upon its completion in 1934 set out on a world cruise chaperoned by Paulette's mother. Their marriage was not confirmed until 1942, when the couple were divorced. According to the records sworn to at the time, they were married in Canton, China, in 1936. In the meantime she had appeared in his next production, *The Great Dictator* (1940).

Shortly after the Chaplins were divorced Paulette wed Burgess Meredith in a ceremony held in the garden of the late David O. Selznick.

During her marriage to Chaplin, Paulette had advanced her career and her bank account by shrewdly negotiated contracts, and her appearance in some important films: *The Cat and the Canary* (1939), *The Women* (1940), *Northwest Mounted Police* (1940), and *Reap the Wild Wind* (1942). Right up until it was announced that Vivien Leigh had been chosen to play the role of Scarlett O'Hara, Hollywood was all but certain that the part in *Gone With the Wind* would go to Miss Goddard.

The Burgess-Goddard liaison lasted five years. During this period the actress continued to star in such big pictures as *Kitty* (1946) and *Unconquered* (1947).

The "girl on the moon," as she was called during her time with Ziegfeld, began to fade in pictures in the early fifties. Some of her last were memorable for their ludicrous titles (which befitted their plots): *Bride of Vengeance* (1949) and *Babes in Baghdad* (1952).

In 1957 the novelist Erich Maria Remarque dedicated his book *The Black Obelisk* to her, and the following year they were married. They maintain apartments in Paris and New York—two in each city because they have not lived together since becoming man and wife.

Paulette, bedecked in part of her famous jewel collection, is a familiar face in chic restaurants and nightclubs in Paris and New York, where she spends most of her time, though in 1966 she appeared as the mother of Claudia Cardinale in the film *Time of Indifference*, from the Alberto Moravia novel.

As she appears today.

Marcelle Corday comforts Luise after the famous telephone scene in *The Great Ziegfeld*, 1936.

LUISE RAINER

Although the Viennese actress was only twenty-two when Metro-Goldwyn-Mayer brought her to Hollywood, Luise Rainer had had practical experience on the stages of Austria since she was four years old. Her debut in films was in 1935 with William Powell in *Escapade*. The audience reaction to her was very favorable, and the front office ordered the scenario department to seek vehicles that would suit her.

Luise was beautiful, talented, and charming, but also extremely mannered. Finding the right part for her was no easy matter. That the studio was able to come up with two parts in the next two years that were perfect makes her story all the more incredible.

She was chosen the Best Actress of 1936 by the Motion Picture Academy for her performance in *The Great Ziegfeld*. Her part was a very small one. She portrayed the late Anna Held in a telephone scene which not only was the dramatic highlight of the film because she made it so, but it was—and is—still referred to—a perfect example of how a good actress with a single prop can run away with a picture.

In the picture with her was William Powell as Flo Ziegfeld, and a large number of stars who had appeared for the great producer in shows over the years, all playing themselves. One was the dancer Ann Pennington, for many years a star on Broadway and famous for her dimpled knees. She lives in a Times Square Hotel not far from the theatres which used to carry her name in blazing lights.

It was *The Good Earth* with Paul Muni in 1937 that enabled Luise Rainer to become the first woman to win the Best Actress award two years in a row. It is a record that has never been equaled by any actress. The picture was the last film made by Irving Thalberg, who died before it was completed. Ironically, it was Thalberg's widow, Norma Shearer, who was favored to win the Oscar that evening for her role in *Romeo and*

Juliet. Miss Rainer was phoned from the hotel where the awards dinner was held and asked to come at once to accept the statuette.

The Culver City lot, thrilled by the publicity and prestige Luise Rainer had brought, put her to work at once in one film after another in an effort to cash in on her box-office potential. Her film *The Emperor's Candlesticks* (1937) was neither well received nor well attended. *Toy Wife* in 1938 was even worse. Both she and Spencer Tracy had to endure the silly plot of *The Big City* (1937). Her only picture of any consequence after the Oscars was *The Great Waltz* in 1938. Based loosely on the life of the Waltz King, Strauss was played by Fernand Gravet, who is still active in the French theatre. His mistress was played by the Polish soprano Miliza Korjus who received an Academy Award nomination that year and then slipped into total obscurity. Miliza is married to a Beverly Hills doctor and has recently begun to make new recordings for her own company, Venus Records.

The downward trend of the Rainer career has been founded on reasons ranging from studio politics to bad advice from playwright Clifford Odets, her husband at the time. Whatever the reason or reasons, the simple and amazing fact is that by 1939 she was finished in Hollywood.

In the early forties she appeared on a number of radio dramatic shows, and in 1942 was seen on Broadway in a play entitled *A Kiss for Cinderella.* Casting Luise Rainer was, however, as difficult in other media as it had been for motion pictures. Her forte was crying scenes, endurance of pain. These unique abilities earned her the titles of "The Viennese Teardrop" and "Austrian Whine."

After over twenty years of inactivity she has shown some interest in acting again. She came all the way from London where she lives with her husband, a prominent publisher, to film a half-hour television play in Hollywood in 1966 because the part interested her. Her leading man was another discard of M-G-M from thirty years ago, Ramon Novarro. The press questioned her upon her arrival about a comeback, but she insists that she prefers the quiet life she leads in England.

A scene from a recent television appearance. *ABC TV*

The First Lady of M-G-M in the mid-1930's.

NORMA SHEARER

Because of the many important pictures she made during the thirties Norma Shearer is usually thought of essentially as a talkie star. She was, however, a big star during the silent era also and appeared in *The Student Prince* (1927) opposite Ramon Novarro and with Lon Chaney in *He Who Gets Slapped* (1924).

Before Norma made a name in Hollywood she did bit parts as far back as 1920, after arriving from her native Canada, in such films as D. W. Griffith's *Way Down East* and *The Flapper*.

Her marriage in 1927 to Irving Thalberg, the boy wonder of the movie industry, assured her of the best vehicles and promotion Metro-Goldwyn-Mayer could offer, which was in fact the best in Hollywood. Her appearance in a film brought out the best in that studio's talents. She was gowned by Adrian. Her sets were provided by Cedric Gibbons, and in later years her brother, Douglas Shearer, supplied the best sound recording in the industry. Her directors, George Cukor, Robert Z. Leonard, and Sidney Franklin, were always the hottest around at the time.

Soon Norma Shearer had the unofficial title of "First Lady of M-G-M." If anyone thought that it was no more than a title they had only to ask other contract actresses such as Joan Crawford and Greta Garbo about who had the choice of roles and pictures during those years.

Wisely, Norma would not allow herself to be typecast. She played everything from high comedy to Shakespeare to Eugene O'Neill.

Norma Shearer was a contender five times for the Academy Award. She received the coveted trophy as the Best Actress of 1929–30 for her performance in *The Divorcee,* and was nominated for her performances in *A Free Soul* (1930–31), *The Barretts of Wimpole Street* (1934), *Romeo and Juliet* (1936), and *Marie Antoinette* (1938).

Thalberg died in 1936, but his widow continued taking the plum roles on the Metro lot. The pictures in which she appeared read like a list of the top productions of the thirties: *Private Lives* (1931), *Strange Interlude* (1932), *The Women* (1939), and *Idiot's Delight* (1939).

In 1942 Miss Shearer made *Her Cardboard Lover.* It was her worst film and it was her last. She announced her retirement from the screen, and has turned thumbs down on such comeback vehicles as *Mrs. Miniver* and *Sunset Boulevard.*

The same year Norma quit acting she married ski instructor Martin Arrouge, a handsome Basque twenty years her junior. Until 1960 they lived in the same huge beach house right on the Pacific Ocean in Santa Monica that she and Thalberg had occupied. Their new home in West Hollywood is the setting for many parties which are attended by Hollywood's Old Guard. Mr. Arrouge was instrumental in bringing the Winter Olympics to Squaw Valley in 1960.

Mrs. Martin Arrouge today, better known as Norma Shearer.

During the early 1930's,
at the height of his fame.

RAMON NOVARRO

Ramon Samaniegoes (his real name) was born in 1899 in Durango, Mexico. Although it was never mentioned in the biographies put out by his studio, Novarro's first film was not *Prisoner of Zenda* in 1922. He had a small role in a Mack Sennett picture in 1921 called *Small Town Idol*. Even before that he played an extra in a Paramount picture in 1919 entitled *The Goat*. He and the late Wallace Beery made their film debuts together under Cecil B. de Mille's direction in a Mary Pickford starrer in 1918, *The Little American*.

Although he made important features such as *The Student Prince* (1925) and *Where the Pavement Ends* (1923), Novarro is best remembered for the title role he played in the 1926 version of *Ben-Hur*. It gave his career an enormous boost, and assured him of screen immortality, but at the same time obscured some of his other outstanding silents, *Scaramouch* (1922) and *The Midshipman* (1925).

Ramon is treated much more kindly today by film buffs and critics than he was by the studios of the twenties—despite consistently good performances and a large, loyal following, he was constantly referred to as "the second Valentino."

Ironically, unlike Rudolph Valentino, he was not limited to playing Latin lovers. (The other giant of the time who overshadowed him in the silent era, John Gilbert, did not survive the advent of sound.) It was a great accomplishment for Novarro finally to convince the producers that he was a star in his own right and to give him vehicles better than embarrassing copies of Valentino pictures, such as *The Arab* (1924).

When talkies arrived his accent was a help rather than a hindrance. M-G-M wisely had him record "Pagan Love Song," the "Moon River" of its day, which was enormously popular. In casting Novarro M-G-M gave him parts that suited a foreign dialect. In 1930 the studio let him play what he actually was, a Spaniard, opposite Dorothy Jordan in *In Gay Madrid*. He played an Oriental with Helen Hayes in *Son-Daughter* (1932), and in *Mata Hari* (1932) he played a Russian opposite Greta Garbo, to whom he posed the famous question, "What is the matter, Mata?" His role in *The Barbarian* (1933) with Myrna Loy was of lesser importance but is an example of how he gracefully made the transition from silents to sound by playing exotic roles. In 1934 he was matched with a countrywoman, Lupe Velez, in *Laughing Boy*.

Ramon has never completely stopped making films, but his roles after *Cat and the Fiddle* (1934) kept getting smaller and smaller. Even when he was given star billing, as in *Desperate Adventure* (1938), it was in a low-budget feature for Republic Pictures.

In the late forties he began turning up again in pictures. His role in *We Were Strangers* (1949) with John Garfield and Jennifer Jones was his largest and most interesting in many years and started talk of a comeback, which never materialized, appearing thereafter in such undistinguished films as *Crisis* (1950) which starred Cary Grant, and *The Outriders* (1950). In 1960 he had a role in *Heller in Pink Tights*.

Novarro never married and lives alone in a large home in the Hollywood Hills. Two consolations he has had over the past years for the descent of his star are his Roman Catholic faith and the money which he wisely invested during his peak years. In August, 1966, Novarro filed a $57,000,000 claim against the United States for rent that he says is due him on that portion of territory around the Rio Grande that the United States returned to Mexico in 1963. The land had been given to Novarro's grandfather by Mexican President Juarez. Because of the change of course of the Rio Grande in 1864 the property was occupied by the United States.

Occasionally he accepts a role on a television show if it seems right to him. He enjoys the medium which in his judgment differs greatly from feature films. During the 1966 season he was seen both with Luise Rainer playing a European nobleman, and as a foreign doctor on *Dr. Kildare*.

As he appears today.

An M-G-M publicity still of Miss Massey which appeared in a movie fan magazine in 1939.

ILONA MASSEY

The Hungarian stage and screen beauty was born in Budapest in 1914. Under her real name, Ilona Hajmassy, she sang in music halls and operettas in Austria, Germany, and Hungary until the mid-thirties when Metro-Goldwyn-Mayer brought her to Hollywood.

M-G-M at the time had under contract Nelson Eddy and Jeanette Mac-Donald, who made some of the top grossing pictures of the period. The fact that they performed together better than they got along personally was an open secret in Hollywood. It was the practice of the majors at that time to have someone waiting in the wings who could fill in for a leading star in case that personality became too difficult. In addition, Metro saw great potential in Ilona as a star in her own right. She could sing beautifully and wore period costumes very well—and was the perfect threat to hold over the head of Jeanette MacDonald.

Nelson Eddy and Ilona Massey were tried as a duo in two movies: *Rosalie* (1937), and *Balalaika* (1939). The public, which had grown used to seeing Eddy with Miss MacDonald, would not accept the new combination that seemed tantamount to adultery. Despite the MacDonald-Eddy feuds being leaked to the press on several occasions, many of their fans actually believed the couple were married.

In 1941 Ilona made a film with Binnie Barnes (wife of Columbia Pictures executive Mike Frankovitch) which was appropriately called *New Wine*. (As any connoisseur will testify, new wine is always very bad.)

During the Second World War Miss Massey was always in danger of some kind—both the F.B.I. and Scotland Yard were after her in *International Lady* (1941) but things turned out all right when the F.B.I. agent, George Brent (retired in Rancho Santa Fe, California), fell in love with her;

she had more problems in *Invisible Agent* (1942) but Jon Hall (living in semi-retirement in Malibu, California) was there to help her, and Bela Lugosi and Lon Chaney, Jr., menaced her in *Frankenstein Meets the Wolfman* (1943). Also in 1943 as a change of pace Ilona Massey sang and clowned with Milton Berle and Arthur Treacher in *Ziegfeld Follies* on Broadway.

Other film credits include: *Holiday in Mexico* (1946) with Jane Powell and Walter Pidgeon, *The Gentleman Misbehaves* (1946), *Northwest Outpost* (1947), another try with Nelson Eddy, *Love Happy* (1950) with the Marx Brothers and her last film *Jet Over the Atlantic* (1959).

When in 1954 a special subcommittee of the House of Representatives held hearings in Manhattan on communist aggression in Eastern Europe, their star witness was the blonde, who testified to the rape, murder, and robbery committed by the Soviets against her people in her native land. Miss Massey had succeeded in bringing some of her family to the United States, but her hatred of Communists is still intense. During the visits of former Premier Nikita Khrushchev and Deputy Premier Anastas Mikoyan to this country in 1959 Ilona Massey was one of those who picketed in protest wherever the Soviet leaders made public appearances, and posed proudly for newspaper cameramen next to signs calling Khrushchev "The Butcher of Bucharest." She is a strong supporter of the Assembly of Captive European Nations and the Hungarian Freedom Fighters.

Ilona has been married successively to Alan Curtis, star of "B" pictures during the forties; to Charles Walker, owner of a fashionable Manhattan jewelry shop, and is now the wife of General Donald S. Dawson. They live in a beautiful home in Bethesda, Maryland, a few miles from the nation's capital where Ilona is both very much a part of the social scene and active in the Reserve Officers Wives' Club and though not a member of course, the Daughters of the American Revolution.

She seems to have little interest in working again in motion pictures or on the stage.

Ilona today.

In a publicity shot published in *Photoplay Magazine*, 1923.

DAGMAR GODOWSKY

While Artur Rubinstein and Leopold Godowsky played a duet in the drawing room, Dagmar Godowsky, silent film vamp, was ushered into the world in the bedroom of a Chicago hotel suite in 1897. Her father, one of the half dozen great pianists of this country, was concertizing in the United States at the time. Shortly after the birth of his daughter he accepted the position of Imperial Royal Professor of Music from Franz Josef, Emperor of Austria-Hungary, and took his family to live in Vienna.

Dagmar was brought up in a home in which the family physician was Dr. Wilhelm Stekel (disciple of Freud), and dinner guests might be Ignace Paderewski, Thomas Mann, Sergei Rachmaninoff or Gustav Mahler.

At the outbreak of World War I the Godowskys moved to the United States, settling in Santa Monica, California. Motion pictures were just beginning to come into their own, and Dagmar, who had recently discovered that she was attractive to men, embarked on a career as a vamp in movies.

She appeared in *The Trap* (1919) and her friend Alla Nazimova gave her a small role in *Stronger Than Death* (1920). She made *Red Lights* (1921), *The Altar Stairs* (1922), *The Peddler of Lies* (1922) with her leading man Frank Mayo, whom she married, *Common Law* (1923), and was given the third female lead in the Valentino starrer, *The Sainted Devil* (1923), and her last film, *Meddling Women* (1924), with Lionel Barrymore.

After two years of marriage she obtained a legal separation, but continued to live in the same house with Mayo under an arrangement Dagmar calls "a platonic marriage," but within a couple of years they were divorced. Mayo died in California in 1963 at the age of seventy-three.

Miss Godowsky then set off for New York where she had a brief run in the Ivor Novello-Constance Collier play *The Rat*, canceled on opening night because of Dagmar's encounter with a bottle of bootleg gin. Following that, under Mark Hellinger's management, she toured the Keith vaudeville circuit in the late twenties doing a dramatic sketch, and made an unsuccessful attempt to run a nightclub in Long Island, New York.

Although she was once described by a cinema magazine as "at her movie most, a minor vamp of the early twenties," her impact on the film colony during those years seems to have been considerable. She claims that it was she who introduced Rudolph Valentino to the late Natacha Rambova, that Charlie Chaplin really wanted to marry her when he was tricked into marrying Mildred Harris, and that Irving Thalberg while still little more than a clerk at Universal was nursed through illnesses with the chicken soup she made for him. During her short career in pictures she played with Helen Keller, Sessue Hayakawa, Nita Naldi, Marie Dressler, and Lon Chaney.

During the thirties she accompanied her father through the Orient, Europe, and South America on his concert tours until his death in 1938. About this time her younger brother, Leo, had developed a process for color photography, which he sold for several million dollars to the Eastman Kodak Company. We know it today as Kodachrome.

For several years Dagmar acted as personal manager for her old friend, Igor Stravinsky. In 1958 she wrote her autobiography, *First Person Plural,* in which she described herself as having been unbelievably beautiful and overwhelmingly charming. Heinrich Ivan Kuchenmeister, the powerful German industrialist, was sufficiently enamoured with Dagmar to offer to leave his wife and risk his professional career for her. At the time, a German aristocrat marrying the daughter of a world-famous Jewish family would be risking both economic and social reprisals. Hitler had just come to power and made it clear that the Jewish presence in the Third Reich was not desired. Dagmar left Germany learning later that the man she seriously considered marrying had become a Nazi. Although the book's accuracy was challenged by many, most critics agreed that it was by far the best written and most amusing of its kind.

During World War II Miss Godowsky held court in a beautiful home in Beverly Hills. She entertained politicians, her old friends from the movie colony, and the giants of the music world.

Madame Godowsky keeps an apartment in Manhattan which she deserts for Europe each summer, also taking an occasional Hollywood jaunt. Some of her close friends are David Sarnoff, Dr. Lin Yutang, Vladimir Horowitz, and the Soviet pianist Sviatoslav Richter. Since the success of her first book she has been promising friends and her publisher to do another. The title will be *I Lose Everything But Weight.*

In New York City recently.
Peter Basch

In 1923, the top comedienne on the screen, and (*below*) photographed recently in a New York hotel lobby.

CONSTANCE TALMADGE

Constance, the youngest of the three famous actress sisters, was born in Brooklyn, New York, in 1900. As a teenage girl she had beautiful brown eyes, golden hair, and one of the most aggressive stage mothers movie executives ever encountered.

Connie did extra work and bit parts in films, such as *Latin Quarter* (1914), before she got the chance to play the mountain girl in D. W. Griffith's masterpiece, *Intolerance* (1916). It was a small role and no one had ever heard of her. When it was shown in theatres, however, the part seemed much more important, a credit to Miss Talmadge's superb flair for comedy. Her next appearance was in the 14-reel epic listed as *Georgia Pearce,* a medieval French story. Two others who were to emerge as stars of the silent era, Bessie Love and Carmel Myers, appeared briefly in the film. Miss Love now lives in Bayswater, England, and Carmel Myers, a New York toiletries manufacturer, claims that she had not made any picture at that time, although one of those who recognized her at a recent screening of the film was her daughter.

Through the energetic pursuit of people in the right places, Mrs. Talmadge was quick to capitalize on the reception her daughter got from the critics and public. In 1917 Connie starred with Earle Foxe in *Honeymoon* and in 1918 she was seen in *The Gray Chiffon Veil.*

Although she made pictures for First National, Selznick, Paramount-Famous Players, and others, Connie's largest group of films were produced by Joseph M. Schenck, husband of her eldest sister Norma. Norma was the Bette Davis of the silent era and was a star second in importance only to Mary Pickford. At the peak of their careers Norma received $8,000 a week and Constance $6,000—with no income tax—making comedy less profitable than drama. The Talmadge girls were what today one calls "super stars." Their name alone assured the financial success of a picture.

Connie was unexcelled during the twenties for sophisticated screen comedy, and was very popular among schoolgirls, who copied her hair styles and clothes. It was a time of fads, and movie stars exaggerated the nonsense to match everything else in their lives. Connie and her friend Aileen Pringle once went on a corn binge for several weeks. Corn chowder, corn fritters, corn on the cob—they couldn't get enough.

Some of the many, many comedies Connie Talmadge is remembered for are: *Wedding Bells* (1921), *Lessons in Love* (1921), and *East Is West* (1922), both from New York stage plays, *Dulcy* (1923), *The Goldfish* (1924), *Heart Trouble* (1924) with Ronald Colman, *Sybil* (1926) with Chester Conklin and *Venus of Venice* (1927).

When talkies came Constance Talmadge went. Unlike her sister Norma, she didn't even try to make the change, and warned the other star against it. But Norma tried sound films, and after a brief success, and failure, she too quit. However, through Mother Talmadge and Norma's husband, the two stars remained among the richest in Hollywood. The Talmadge studios where their productions were made is now a studio of a West Hollywood decorator and set designer. The dressing rooms of the two sisters have been for years an apartment house inhabited by Estelle Winwood, famous actress of *The Madwoman of Chaillot*, among others.

Since her retirement Constance has lived quietly in her homes in Hollywood and New York. She maintains an apartment on Manhattan's Park Avenue not far from that of two other silent stars, Lillian Walker and Olga Baclanova. She is still close to her sister Natalie, who was known more as the wife of Buster Keaton than as a movie actress. Natalie lives in Santa Monica, California, a short distance from Mary Miles Minter, who has refused to be photographed, interviewed, or even to give an autograph since her career was ruined following the murder in 1922 of William Desmond Taylor, the silent screen director.

Connie has been married to John Pialoglou, Alistair McIntosh, and Townsend Netcher, and was widowed by her last husband, Wally Giblin, a Wall Street broker.

John Virzi

From left to right: Connee, Martha, and Vet Boswell at the height of their popularity, 1934. *Paul Schaeffer*

THE BOSWELL SISTERS

The Boswell Sisters, Connee (originally Connie), Vet (Helvetia), and Martha, hailed from New Orleans, Louisiana, where they began playing instruments and singing before they were of school age. They had been playing clubs around the country in the twenties before swing was the popular sound (with the exception of a few musicians). Their first record was made in 1928 for Victor (before it became RCA Victor). Two of their early hits of 1930 and 1931 were "My Future Just Passed" and "When I Take My Sugar to Tea."

"The Boswell Sound," as it is still called in the music business, created a sensation. There had been sister acts before, and many since, but it was these three Southern girls who were able to blend their voices in a way the public never heard before—they merged harmony, rhythm, and feeling to produce a musical togetherness that has been imitated but never equaled. The records they made during the thirties for the Brunswick and Okeh labels are among the most highly prized and sought-after by discophiles.

In 1930 they had a popular radio program for Camel Cigarettes, and the next year were regulars with Bing Crosby on *The Woodbury Hour*. In 1932 the Boswells were heard on Chesterfield Cigarettes' *Music That Satisfies* show. The announcer was Norman Brokenshire. All of these shows were on NBC's Red Network, and when in 1933 the girls moved over to rival CBS it was considered a major coup for Bill Paley's network, which until that time had been unsuccessful in its competition with NBC for big name talent. From then on the announcers started saying with much more authority, "This is CBS, the stars' address."

Truly musicians' musicians, the group has been praised by the top performers of their time—and since. No lesser names than Bing Crosby, Ella

Fitzgerald, and Paul Whiteman expressed admiration for the distinct qualities of their sound. Rudy Vallee was one of the earliest Boswell enthusiasts. Not only did the girls sing great but each was also an accomplished instrumentalist as well. Connee, who has been confined to a wheel chair since she suffered a polio attack at the age of three, plays just about every instrument but favors the saxaphone. Martha was usually on piano, and Vet alternated between banjo and violin.

The girls appeared together in three pictures. In 1932 they made both *Moulin Rouge* with Constance Bennett and Franchot Tone and *The Big Broadcast* with Kate Smith, Burns and Allen, and Bing Crosby. In 1934 they were in *Transatlantic Merry-Go-Round* with the late Nancy Carroll.

When Vet and Martha decided to give up show business for marriage in 1936 the team broke up. Connee, the youngest, who had been appearing as a single as well as with her sisters since the beginning, continued alone.

During the Second World War when she was entertaining troops and had to sign hundreds of autographs every day she began spelling her name "ee" instead of the original "Connie."

She has appeared recently at the Flamingo and Thunderbird hotels in Las Vegas, in New Orleans at the Hotel Roosevelt, and in New York City on *The Ed Sullivan Show* and *Perry Como Show*. Connee has been married since 1935 to Harry Leedy, who managed the sisters since they began performing professionally. They live in a large apartment on New York's Central Park West full of the paintings Connee does in her spare time.

Martha lived on a farm near Peekskill, New York, until her death in 1958. She had one son.

Vet, the second eldest of the trio, has been residing in Peekskill with her husband, who died in 1958, and daughter. Mrs. John P. Jones (her name by marriage) manages to get to the city for a visit with Connee about once a month. If the deal now pending to film the Boswell sisters' biographies goes through she will dub the musical sequences with her sister.

Two contemporaries they still see are Morton Downey and Gene Austin, famous popular singers. Downey is a director of a number of corporations living in Stamford, Connecticut, and Austin still plays a nightclub engagement now and then and resides in Las Vegas.

Connee and Vet posed recently for the only photograph taken of them together since the sister act was dissolved in 1936. *Edward Oleksak*

As "Baron von Munchausen"
in the early 1930's. *NBC*

JACK PEARL

Jack Pearl is one of the last and one of the greatest of a vanishing breed in show business—the dialect comedian. Over twenty years have passed since his heyday, and yet even now young people, who are completely unaware of the real Baron von Munchausen and the self-styled Munchausen, Jack Pearl, are still posing the famous question, "Vas You Dare, Sharlie?"

In 1932 when *One Man's Family* began and Jack Benny made his first broadcast, Jack Pearl was already one of radio's biggest hits. An example of just how fast and firmly he caught on is shown by his salary, which Lucky Strike Cigarettes raised from $3,500 to $8,500 weekly, in only five months. The absurd lies of "Baron von Munchausen" and news from his famous "Cousin Hoogo" kept audiences howling from coast to coast during the crippling Depression.

Pearl was not, however, a name made by radio. He began his career as one of the many young people who were at one time members of Gus Edwards' famous "School Days" act in vaudeville. Some of his classmates were George Jessel, Walter Winchell, and Ricardo Cortez, who is now a New York stockbroker. After his graduation to adult roles he performed in many revues, plays, and musicals on Broadway, and was many times on the bill at the prestigious Palace, the cathedral of Vaudeville. In 1927 he and Ted Lewis were starred in *Artists and Models* on Broadway. Pearl was chosen to star in the last *Ziegfeld Follies* (1931) that was personally produced by the great showman. With him in that show were Harry Richman, the late Helen Morgan, and Ruth Etting. It was the show from which Miss Etting was dropped because of a dispute between Flo Ziegfeld and her manager-husband, Moe "the Gimp" Snyder. Etting and her present husband, Myrle Alderman, are living quietly in Colorado Springs, Colorado. Moe Snyder is a businessman in his hometown, Chicago.

The character, Baron von Munchausen, became so popular that when Pearl made movies he received second billing to the Baron. One film utilized the fictitious nobleman in the title *Meet the Baron* (M-G-M, 1933), with the credits reading, "Jack Pearl as 'Baron von Munchausen.'" Costarring with him were Jimmy Durante and the late Zasu Pitts.

By the time TV came on the scene producers and networks had become increasingly cautious of comedians who told jokes in ethnic accents. Pearl, who had always been a welcome guest on the biggest shows of the thirties and forties, was offered shots on such programs as the *Ed Sullivan Show* on TV, but the censors were becoming increasingly nervous over his material. The irony of the change in standards for comedy is galling to Pearl. Never in his career was he accused of being "blue" and yet material is now permitted on television and radio that would have brought the vice squad, while dialects of Jews, Germans, Negroes, etc., are frowned upon as being offensive.

For a while he tried turning to dramatic acting, but there was little interest in his availability as an actor. "They'll let Berle, Jessel, Gleason, and Ed Wynn do serious bits but not Jack Pearl. I don't know what it is. I don't beef about not working. Thank God, I don't need to for the money anymore. I withdrew my services except as an actor, and it looks like they don't want me on those terms."

Jack lives in the East Fifties in New York City. He still keeps in touch with many of the great stars he knew and worked with in his prime. Two of his close Manhattan friends are the legendary comedy team Smith and Dale.

Asked if he resented the fact that the Baron became more famous than he, Pearl replies: "I didn't when the money was coming in, but I've got to admit that sometimes even now it bothers me a little. After all these years I get cab drivers who'll turn around and say, 'Hey, aren't you the guy who used to play the Baron?' But listen, I'm grateful, too, that they remember."

Jack Pearl today: retired.
John Virzi

Fan letters sent to her radio series during the thirties and forties were replied to with this photograph.

IRENE RICH

The popular radio and screen star was born of prosperous parents in Buffalo, New York, in 1891. While Irene was still young the family moved West after losing most of their money in a financial panic. Before entering films as an extra in 1918, Irene worked as a real-estate saleswoman.

Her first real part that year was in *The Girl in His House,* in which she had the second lead. In 1919 she was with Lon Chaney in *The Trap,* and the following year made the first of several movies with Will Rogers, *Jes' Call Me Jim.* In 1921 she made *Desperate Trails* with Harry Carey, and in 1922 played second fiddle to the star of *Brawn of the North*—Strongheart, the famous movie dog. One of Irene's most famous silents was *Lady Windemere's Fan* in 1925.

Although Miss Rich has described her screen image as "the doormat in an endless series of domestic films," she departed from that character in 1928 to essay the role of Harriet Craig in the original screen version of the prize-winning play *Craig's Wife.*

She realized her appeal was to women rather than men and chose her screen roles and her later radio scripts accordingly. Irene Rich made pictures for Warner, Fox, Goldwyn, Universal, and Pathé before the advent of sound films and afterwards went from Metro-Goldwyn-Mayer to Republic and back again.

In 1933 Irene Rich began her coast-to-coast radio program entitled *Dear John.* It was an immediate success. In 1936 *Variety* called her "The No. 1 Slim Woman of the Air," referring to her claim that it was her sponsor's product that kept her slender. Her sponsor, Welch's Grape Juice, claimed that his sales had increased 638 percent since the show began. Some of the "Dear John" scripts were written by Arch Oboler.

To promote the series and the product Miss Rich's age became one of the best documented in America. In newspaper, magazine, and radio advertisements she constantly proclaimed that although she was thirty-nine, those wonderful nonalcoholic grapes had kept her svelte and beautiful. Later it was although she was forty, although she was forty-one, and from then on the age became simply, "over forty." The radio series lasted over a decade, right into the forties.

Her sound career was less successful at its beginning. She made *So This Is London* with Will Rogers, and a few other talkies of little distinction before announcing in 1934 that she had given up Hollywood and the movies.

In 1935 she costarred on Broadway with the late George M. Cohan in *Seven Keys to Baldpate* and did not return to Hollywood until 1938 when she again began playing mothers and grandmothers in such films as *That Certain Age* (1938) with Deanna Durbin, *The Mortal Storm* (1940), and *Keeping Company* (1941) with Ann Rutherford (now Mrs. William Dozier, wife of the producer of TV's *Batman* series).

Some of Miss Rich's other credits are: Down to Earth (1932) with Will Rogers again, *The Lady in Question* (1940) with a very young Rita Hayworth, *Calendar Girl* (1947) supporting Jane Frazee (now Mrs. Tryon, of Santa Monica, California), *Fort Apache* (1948) the epic western, and taking time out in 1948 to costar with the late Bobby Clark on Broadway in *As the Girls Go* before doing one of the biggest critical and financial failures of movie history, the Ingrid Bergman version of *Joan of Arc* (1950).

An astute businesswoman, Irene ran a successful stock farm during her years on radio. She prided herself on the fact that every facet of her business showed a profit. At a time when movie names meant "box office" for personal appearances she was a familiar face on the vaudeville circuits in major cities around the country.

Irene married her fourth husband, George Henry Clifford, a wealthy New York businessman in March, 1950, living at the time in the Waldorf Towers in Manhattan. A few years later they moved to the Hope Ranch in Santa Barbara, California, a kind of senior-citizen project for retired millionaires, which has a beautiful golf course and country club. The Clifford home is set in a lovely wooded area. One of their neighbors is her sculptress daughter, with whom Irene shares her life-time supply of grape juice.

On the grounds of her home recently in Santa Barbara, California. *John Virzi*

BEBE DANIELS

The early screen star was born in 1901 in Dallas, Texas, to theatrical parents who moved to Los Angeles when she was still a baby. Bebe (pronounced "bee-bee") was educated in convent schools and played child roles in silents and for the various stock companies that were located in Los Angeles.

Before appearing in a feature picture Bebe made over 200 shorts with comedians Harold Lloyd and Snub Pollard. While dining one night with Lloyd, Cecil B. de Mille spotted her and offered her a part in *Male and Female* (1919). Some of her other early movies were: *Everywoman* (1919) with Violet Heming (a resident of Manhattan's East 57th Street), *Affairs of Anatol* (1921), *North of the Rio Grande* (1922) with Shannon Day (living in a theatrical hotel in New York City and teaching drama), and the Valentino starrer *Monsieur Beaucaire* (1924) with Doris Kenyon (living in Beverly Hills with her musician husband), *Argentine Lover* (1924) opposite Ricardo Cortez, and *Lovers in Quarantine* (1925) with the stage actor Alfred Lunt.

Even at the beginning, Bebe had the distinction of being liked as much by her colleagues as by her fans. She and Betty Compson (now running a gift shop in Glendale, California) were chosen as the two most popular stars among the stars. In 1920 movie fan magazines conducted a poll among their readers to determine the most popular film folk, and Bebe Daniels was sixth on a list headed by Mary Pickford.

In 1921 the actress was arrested for speeding and sentenced to ten days in jail. Her cell had a Persian rug on the floor, her meals were catered by an elegant restaurant—and her Stutz was parked outside. Musicians serenaded her, and just about every star in Hollywood came to visit her—among the 792 who signed her guest book were Jesse Lasky, Jack Pickford, Eddie Sutherland (now living in a New York hotel while he negotiates old films for TV), and Priscilla Dean (now living in Leonia, New Jersey). As soon as she was released she went into a picture based on her experience, called *The Speed Girl* (1921).

Bebe Daniels was probably the most versatile star in silent films. Paramount Pictures put her in westerns, melodramas, comedies, costume epics, and flapper stories. Until the advent of sound she appeared in pictures such as: *Miss Brewster's Millions* (1926), *Volcano* (1926), *A Kiss in a Taxi* (1927) with Chester Conklin, *Take Me Home* opposite Neil Hamilton, and *Feel My Pulse* (1928) with Richard Arlen.

When her studio refused to believe she could make a successful talkie she bought out her contract and went to RKO where she not only talked but sang in one of the most successful musicals in movie history, *Rio Rita* (1929). After that Bebe was a bigger star than ever and went on to make such sound films as *Dixiana* (1930), another musical, *Reaching for the Moon* (1931) with Bing Crosby in his first important part, *The Maltese Falcon* (1931), *Silver Dollar* (1932), *42nd Street* (1933), and *Counsellor at Law* (1933) with John Barrymore, directed by William Wyler.

Bebe was probably the most eligible bachelor girl in Hollywood and dated such notables as Jack Dempsey, tennis' Bill Tilden, and Rod La Rocque. She changed all that by marrying Ben Lyon on June 14, 1930, with whom she made *Alias French Gertie* (1930). They toured the United States in several plays during the thirties with time out for Bebe to do *The Song You Gave Me* (1933) in England. In 1936 the husband-wife team went to London for a three-week Palladium engagement, which was so successful that they toured the British Isles with the act until 1939, when Ben became the head of the English talent office for Twentieth Century-Fox. Even after World War II broke out the Lyons stayed on in London earning the love and respect of the English people by entertaining servicemen and civilians throughout the Blitz. In 1946 they returned to Hollywood but after a short time there decided that they had truly become Londoners, and moved back again.

In England they made feature films, *Life With the Lyons* (1954) and *The Lyons in Paris* (1956) never released in the U.S. and they had a radio show *Hi, Gang,* which ran 12 years and four years on TV.

Until Bebe had a stroke in 1963 the Lyons were one of the most popular families in England. Miss Daniels has nearly completely recovered from her illness, but is still advised by doctors not to become involved in anything that requires too much work. She is now trying her hand at writing mystery stories.

In 1926 Miss Daniels was the "good little bad girl"—playing both heroine and heavy. At the right are Ben, Bebe, and son Richard, adopted war orphan. He played Irene Dunne's boy in *Anna and the King of Siam,* and is one of London's top disc jockeys. *British Broadcasting Corporation*

Stepin worked up enough energy to lift a finger in *Charlie Chan in Egypt* (1935).

STEPIN FETCHIT

The first Negro actor to receive featured billing in movies was born in Key West, Florida, in 1902. His real name is Lincoln Theodore Perry. Little is known about his early years before reaching Hollywood, in the late twenties. He claims to have had stage experience, but no credits have ever been offered.

Stepin Fetchit fell right into the caricature created by "Amos 'n' Andy"— the Negro as funnyman. As for Stepin, he walked, talked, and thought seemingly in slow motion, and was particularly popular with audiences in spooky pictures, where the slightest creak of a floorboard would set his eyes rolling and his knees shaking.

The way in which he was treated by his friend Will Rogers in pictures they made together is a study in race relations of the period. It was perfectly acceptable for the greatly respected comedian to talk to Fetchit in much the same manner that one would address a not too bright house pet, and threats of a kick in the pants to get Stepin moving sent the audience into hysterics. With his eyes always half closed and his slue-foot gait, Fetchit played to a fare-thee-well the stereotype of the southern field hand. His delivery was very much like that of the Amos 'n' Andy character, "Lightnin'."

Although many Negroes had appeared in pictures before his arrival, Stepin Fetchit was the first to register on the screen as a personality. In the early thirties he was placed under contract to Fox Films, and set about living like a movie star—or at least as he thought a movie star should live. By his own count he owned 16 different automobiles during the decade of the thirties. One was a pink Rolls Royce, which he claims was the first in Hollywood, and no one yet has challenged his statement; another was a Cadillac limousine with a white chauffeur. His favorite automobile had a neon sign with his name across the back of it. Stepin also owned two dozen custom-made suits and 50 shirts.

He has stated that he made over $2 million, and while it is doubtful that his contract and free-lancing could have brought that much, he worked a great deal, and certainly would have done very well. The fact that the money was made at a time when prices were less than half what they are

194

today makes his plight all the sadder—he declared bankruptcy in Chicago in 1947, with assets of $146.

Some of the films in which he appeared are: *Swing High* (1930) with the late Helen Twelvetrees, *Carolina* (1934) which starred Janet Gaynor, *The World Moves On* (1934) with Madeleine Carroll (now dividing her time between New York and Paris), *Judge Priest* (1934) with Will Rogers, *Country Chairman* (1935) and *Steamboat Round the Bend* (1935) both with Will Rogers. Stepin played the role of Joe in *Showboat* (1936) and was with Charlie Ruggles in *His Exciting Night* (1938).

In 1943 a judge in Chicago sentenced him to thirty days in jail for impairing the morals of a minor. It was during a period when he was working at small clubs and carnivals around the country in a review called *Flamingo Follies*. It was rumored that he could not find work in films because the civil rights groups objected to his portraying the Negro in an offensive manner. When asked about this Stepin said that he changed his image and his act long ago, but that people just haven't noticed the difference. He seemed to resent people associating him with "Uncle Tom," and yet in 1951 he ran an ad in *Variety* billing himself as "The Laziest Man in the World." His counterpart, Butterfly McQueen, now works about in Atlanta.

His last films were made after a hiatus of nearly 15 years. He was with Jimmy Stewart in *Bend of the River* (1952), and appeared in the Joan Crawford picture *Sudden Fear* (1954).

In 1964 Fetchit was admitted as a charity patient to the Cook County Hospital in Chicago for a prostate operation. Nothing more was heard of him until Heavyweight Champion of the World Cassius Clay, after knocking out Sonny Liston in Maine in May, 1965, announced he did it with a punch taught him by his good friend Stepin Fetchit. The former character actor was on hand to explain to reporters that he had learned the "secret punch" from another Negro champion, Jack Johnson.

It would be difficult to find a more incongruous situation than the Clay-Fetchit association. The world's perhaps most famous and most arrogant Negro, Cassius Clay, has among his entourage the Negro who probably has done more than any man today to label his race with all the things Clay isn't. If there is justification for the relationship, it is probably Stepin's conversion to the Black Muslim faith.

Sampling a piece of his birthday cake recently, served by his old friend Cal Thompson, chef at a Chicago hotel. *Wide World*

MISCHA AUER

The Sad Russian of so many movies in the thirties and forties was born Mischa Ounskowski in 1905. His father was a Czarist naval officer. The family occupied an estate 30 miles from St. Petersburg, and Mischa still remembers being able to see the spires of the churches in the city on clear days. The house and land are now a part of Finland.

After the Bolsheviks took power, Mischa was sent with the children of the Russian intelligentsia to a school in Siberia where they were to learn communism. It was a time of famine, and he became one of the roaming children of Russia—"the original company," says Mischa—who traveled together from place to place seeking food and shelter.

Finally he escaped with his mother to Southern Russia, and became an assistant apothecary to the British Expeditionary Forces, who were stationed there. During this time Mischa drove an ambulance in a typhus plague, and saw his mother die of the disease.

In 1920 his maternal grandfather, Leopold Auer, who had been violin soloist to the Czar, succeeded in bringing him to the United States. He was given the name Auer, and sent to study at New York's Ethical Culture School.

Mischa became very interested in the theatre, and during the twenties was with both Eva Le Gallienne's company and Walter Hampden's. In 1925 he appeared with Helen Chandler on Broadway in a production of *The Wild Duck.*

When talking pictures arrived Hollywood was looking for accents. Mischa went west and spent three years struggling in small parts. His early period in films includes: *The Benson Murder Case* (1930), *Women Love Once* (1931) with Lilyan Tashman, *Unholy Garden* (1931), a Ronald Colman starrer, *Arsene Lupin* (1932) with both John and Lionel Barrymore, *Mata Hari* (1932) with Greta Garbo, *The Infernal Machine* (1933), and *The Crusades* (1935). In most of them he played the heavy.

Then in 1936 his career took a sharp turn upward when director Gregory La Cava cast Mischa as the character who impersonates a gorilla in *My Man Godfrey.* He was nominated for that year's Oscar as the Best Supporting Actor and, although he didn't win, it meant the end of his menace period.

A few of the forty-odd films the Russian made after *Godfrey* are: *That Girl from Paris* (1936) with Lily Pons (semi-retired in Palm Springs, California), *You Can't Take It With You* (1938), *Hellzapoppin* (1941) with Olsen and Johnson, *Twin Beds* (1942), and *Up in Mabel's Room* (1944).

In the forties Auer began devoting most of his time to the stage. In 1941 Mischa and Jessie Matthews (now one of England's most popular soap opera television queens) were in the unsuccessful *The Lady Comes Across.* In 1942 he and his wife, Joyce Hunter, played the Loew's State Theatre on

Broadway in a very successful act with Mischa, assisted by his wife, playing the piano, telling jokes, and doing some wildly funny business with a couple of grapefruits and a lemon. He and Joyce had been married in 1941 with Mayor La Guardia presiding.

Mischa was a great favorite in summer stock, and was seen in *Twentieth Century* in 1948 playing the producer, *The Happy Time* in 1953, and *Room Service,* also in 1953.

His film and stage appearances since then have been rare. In 1958 he played with Martine Carol in the French film *The Foxiest Girl in Paris,* and his last movie to be released in the United States was *We Joined the Navy* (1962). In 1964 he starred in New York in the Lincoln Center State Theatre production of *The Merry Widow.*

Mischa, who speaks English, Russian, German, French, Spanish, and Italian, has been living in various parts of Europe for more than ten years. He moved from Paris to Spain, and after marrying again in 1965, settled down in Rome, where he plays host to visiting Hollywoodites who come away raving about his cooking.

In 1939, the year he costarred with Bing Crosby and Joan Blondell in *East Side of Heaven.*

The Mischa of the present.
Friedman-Abeles

Atlantic City, 1941.

MISS AMERICA OF 1941

At the age of four Rosemary La Planche made her public debut as the bearded daughter of the late Louise Fazenda in the silent film *The Bearded Lady of the Circus*. Later she had supporting roles in two of Deanna Durbin's biggest hits, *100 Men and a Girl* (1936) and *Mad About Music* (1938).

A native Californian, Rosemary was born in the Atwater district of Glendale and attended John Marshall High School. It was during her graduation year that she took the coveted Miss America title. Prior to that she had held the title of "Miss California" for both 1940 and 1941.

Following the Atlantic City coronation (Bert Parks did not do the honors that year), she was signed by RKO Pictures, and eventually appeared in over fifty films, either starring or featured at Columbia, Monogram, and Republic, as well as her home lot. Rosemary's credits include: *The Falcon in Danger* (1943) opposite Tom Conway (discovered in 1965 broke and despondent in a furnished room in Venice, California), *The Sky's the Limit* (1943) with Joan Leslie and Fred Astaire, *The Mexican Spitfire's Blessed Event* (1943) with blonde Marion Martin (now Mrs. Karzykoski of Santa Monica, California), *Two Weeks to Live* (1943) with Lum 'n' Abner, *Prairie Chickens* (1943), *Swing Your Partner* (1943) with Vera Vague (married to Norman Morrell, the associate producer of the Andy Williams TV show), *Betty Co-ed* (1946), *Devil Bat's Daughter* (1946), and *Strangler of the Swamp* (1946).

However, before embarking on her acting career and immediately after winning the coveted title, Rosemary was sent on a whirlwind public appearance tour around the United States. Her first stop was the now-demolished Roxy Theatre in Manhattan where her act consisted of chatting with the emcee and doing a tap dance. One of the burning questions fired at her wherever she went that year by the press was whether or not she approved of the then controversial dance called "the jitterbug." Miss America seemed to please both young and old by saying that she thought it fun to do but admitted that it was rather ugly to watch.

In 1947 Miss America became Mrs. Harry Koplan; her husband was the emcee on various radio and TV shows he produced in Los Angeles. His longest-running show was an audience participation program, on both media, called *Meet the Missus*. Very often Rosemary was part of the entertainment on the shows her husband put together, though they appeared together mostly on KNX, the CBS outlet in Hollywood. Appearing on the same station at the time was a singer from the old Kay Kyser aggregation, Harry Babbitt, who now sells land units in a senior-citizen project in Laguna, California.

Rosemary La Planche's commercials for Cuticura and Geritol are still running on the *Lawrence Welk Show* and *Ted Mack's Amateur Hour* among others, and she has appeared also acting on *The Donna Reed Show, Hennessey, and CBS Reports*.

The Koplans live in Sherman Oaks, California. Rosemary is the mother of a teenage boy and girl (the owners of a turtle, tortoise, and miniature French poodle). The former Miss America, even while raising a family, manages to keep active as an actress. Now that the children are a bit older she is seen on television quite often. She lists her hobbies as cooking, sculpturing, painting, and dancing. Her interest in art has become more than a sideline of late after she sold eight paintings in six months.

She attributes her present slender figure to dancing, a talent which gave her a number of points when she won her title. The judges must have known what they were doing in 1941, when Rosemary's measurements were 36-24-34. They are exactly the same today.

Sherman Oaks, California, today.

In 1941, one of her best years.

JOAN LESLIE

Born Joan Agnes Theresa Sadie Brodell in Detroit, Michigan, in 1925, Joan and her sister Betty were singing and dancing in vaudeville while still in grammar school. While on tour with their act in New York City an MGM talent scout saw Joan and signed her to play Robert Taylor's little sister in the Greta Garbo starrer *Camille* (1937).

Free-lancing between her *Camille* role and her first studio contract, she did *Men With Wings* (1938) in which she supported Andy Devine, *Winter Carnival* (1939) with Virginia Gilmore (a member of New York City's chapter of Alcoholics Anonymous and the ex-wife of Yul Brynner), *Two Thoroughbreds* (1939) with Jimmy Lydon, *Nancy Drew, Reporter* (1940) with Bonita Granville (now Mrs. Jack Wrather of Beverly Hills) and *Laddie* (1940).

Joan used the name Leslie from the very beginning in show business, but changed it briefly to Carmencita Johnson for her role in *High School* (1940) with Jane Withers.

The picture in which she got her big break was *High Sierra* (1941) with Humphrey Bogart. Placed under contract to Warner Brothers, Joan played opposite Gary Cooper and Dickie Moore (now a public relations executive specializing in industrial shows in New York City) in *Sergeant York* (1941), and did two films that year with Eddie Albert: *The Wagons Roll at Night* and *The Great Mr. Nobody*. From then on the studio treated her as the top ingenue on the lot. For her sixteenth birthday Jack Warner gave her a new Buick, and Joan and her family moved to Beverly Hills. But of all the things happening to her, the roles she was being assigned were the best of all.

In 1942 she was seen in two of the finest pictures produced that year: *The Male Animal* and *Yankee Doodle Dandy* singing and dancing along with Jimmy Cagney (who is retired on his farm in Martha's Vineyard,

Massachusetts). In 1943 she had a role in the excellent drama *The Hard Way* in which she played the kid sister of Ida Lupino. Joan was the dancing partner of Fred Astaire in *The Sky's the Limit* (1943) and was Ronald Reagan's girl in *This Is the Army* (1943), an Irving Berlin musical. Again in 1943 Miss Leslie and the late Eddie Cantor teamed up in *Thank Your Lucky Stars*.

In 1945 she began appearing with Robert Hutton, with whom she has remained friends through the years, in a series of films which were very popular at the time—*Too Young to Know* (1945), *Janie Gets Married* (1946), and *Wallflower* (1948).

Joan made two films with Robert Alda, *Rhapsody in Blue* (1945) and *Cinderella Jones* (1946). In 1945 she was loaned to Twentieth Century-Fox for *Where Do We Go From Here?* which had in its cast two players who were to marry years later: Fred MacMurray and June Haver.

During the Second World War Joan Leslie appeared often at defense plants and army bases to entertain the workers and the boys in service. Few Hollywood stars put in as many hours as she did at the famous Hollywood Canteen near Hollywood Boulevard and Vine Street. She was "the girl next door" or, "the girl back home" to tens of thousands of G.I.'s throughout the forties who sent for her photograph.

After her marriage in 1951 to Dr. William Caldwell, Joan found she had less time for and interest in acting. A few years after their twin girls were born she accepted a part in the Vera Hruba Ralston starrer *Jubilee Trail* (1954) at Republic and was seen in *The Revolt of Mamie Stover* (1957) but she still has no interest in a comeback. A few years ago Robert Hutton was visiting Hollywood from England where he was living and asked Joan's permission to submit her name for a running part in a television series he was discussing, but she refused.

Joan, her husband, and her teenage twin girls have been living in a large beautiful house in the Los Feliz area of Los Angeles, where she is active in Catholic charity work.

At a recent party at the Beverly Hilton Hotel in Beverly Hills, California. *John Virzi*

In a scene from one of his early talkies, *The Man I Love* (1929).

RICHARD ARLEN

Richard Arlen, who appeared in the first movie that was named Best Picture of the Year, was born in 1899 in Charlottesville, Virginia. His real name is Richard van Mattimore. During World War I he was a member of the Royal Flying Corps, and after the Armistice attended St. Thomas College in Virginia for a while, moved to St. Paul, Minnesota, where he worked as a sports writer for a newspaper, and was the swimming coach at the St. Paul Athletic Club. Following that, for a brief time he labored in the oil fields in Texas.

Arlen likes to tell the story of how he lived on 14 cents a day for over three weeks after first arriving in Hollywood and making the rounds of the studios. The only job he was able to get in movies was as a worker in a film laboratory at Paramount. He broke his leg one day in an accident on the job, and was sent to the Paramount hospital where he was spotted by a director who promised him a part once he was well again.

Richard's first important role was in 1923 when he played in *Vengeance of the Deep*. Placed under contract to Paramount, he played in a raft of silents throughout the twenties. A few of his early credits are: *Coast of Folly* (1926) opposite Gloria Swanson and *Figures Don't Lie* (1926).

In 1926, after the cameras had been rolling several days on *Volcano*, he was taken off the picture. Feeling that his career had suffered a major set-back he went into a fit of depression. Another contract player, the beautiful actress Jobyna Ralston, was the one to cheer him up. They were married in 1927. That year he appeared in *Blood Ship* costarring Jacqueline Logan, and *Rolled Stockings* with Clara Bow.

Instead of his career going downgrade it went skyward when he won a role in *Wings* (1927), the picture that received the first Academy Award ever given for the Best Picture of the Year. It was directed with great authority by William Wellman, who, like Arlen, had flown during the

202

war, and starred Clara Bow, Gary Cooper, and Charles "Buddy" Rogers (married to Mary Pickford for many years now).

Arlen was in two of the most important early talkies. The first was *Beggars of Life* (1928) which was adapted for the screen from the popular novel of the day, written by Jim Tully. Again Arlen had William Wellman as director, and this time costarred with the American actress who became one of Europe's most popular leading ladies, Louise Brooks (who writes an occasional article for cinema magazines in her home in Rochester, New York). The second was the first talkie version of the classic Western *The Virginian* (1929) with Gary Cooper and Walter Huston. In 1929 he also appeared in *Three Feathers* with Clive Brook, who now lives in England.

Few actors worked more than Arlen during the thirties and forties in sound pictures, a sampling of which are: *Touchdown* (1931) with Charles Starrett (now living in Laguna Beach, California—as do, among other neighbors, Brenda Joyce and Eric Linden), *All American* (1932) opposite Johnny Darrow (now a successful Hollywood talent agent), *Tiger Shark* (1932), *Three-Cornered Moon* (1933), *Alice in Wonderland* (1933) playing the part of the Cheshire Cat and which starred Charlotte Henry (now a secretary in a convent in San Diego, California), *College Humor* (1933) with Mary Carlisle (now managing the Elizabeth Arden salon in Beverly Hills, California), *Helldorado* (1934) with Madge Evans (who, since 1939, has been the wife of the Broadway playwright Sidney Kingsley), *Forced Landing* (1941), *Speed to Spare* (1948), and *Sabre Jet* (1953).

Richard Arlen, who has appeared in over 250 feature films, toured summers during the fifties in *Anniversary Waltz* on the strawhat circuit, and several years later appeared in two movies, *The Best Man* (1964) in a walk-on part, and *Cavalry Command* (1965). For a while in the early sixties he was the representative for Puritan Sweaters in trade shows around the United States.

Arlen, who lives in North Hollywood, is currently on a national lecture tour talking about the Hollywood he has known over the years.

In his San Fernando Valley home recently.
John Virzi

Evelyn Rudie as she appeared on the *Playhouse 90* dramatization of *Eloise* in 1956. *CBS TV*

EVELYN RUDIE

Playing the title role on the *Playhouse 90* TV dramatization of Kay Thompson's *Eloise* was Evelyn Rudie, who had never before had a large part. This was 1956, the time of live television. Miss Rudie was eight years old at the time.

Evelyn got through *Eloise* with splendid notices. Through sheer force of personality and an incredible sense of publicity she emerged more famous than the fictional child. Her press conferences from then on were better attended than those of top stars. It had been many years since Hollywood had a child star, and the press put her on at every opportunity, encouraging her to speak out on every conceivable ill in the world. A precocious little girl, Evelyn needed little prompting.

Evelyn appeared more in the papers during the balance of the fifties than in television and movies. Her personality and image were so strong that it was difficult to cast her though she appeared as a guest on many TV shows, more times than not playing herself, and just about every interviewer around had her on to say something cute.

The only two outstanding bits of work she did at that time were her appearance in the television spectacular, *The Red Mill,* and a movie, *The Gift of Love,* in which she costarred with Lauren Bacall. Both of these were in 1958.

The demise of Evelyn Rudie as an actress and public personality came one year later when the Hollywood police, the Federal Bureau of Investigation, and all the news services were alerted that Evelyn was missing. Hours later she was "found" aboard a plane bound for the nation's capital. Miss Rudie once during a casual meeting with Mamie Eisenhower had been invited to visit the White House. On the spur of the moment, without informing anyone, the moppet decided to take the First Lady up on the invitation.

Almost nothing has been heard of Evelyn since. Her parents insisted that she finish her schooling before accepting any more roles. Even her fan mail is delivered first to her father. She answered a recent note from one:

"About my plans—there is not much to tell yet, except that I'm terribly busy in college. I made straight 'A's (brag, brag) in my last year at Hollywood High School (majoring in science). In my spare time I study dancing, piano (both modern and classical), and acting, of course. I have done quite some stage work recently here in Los Angeles and also given several concerts. Films and TV are tabu for me for the time being, as it would absorb too much time, and my parents want me to go ahead with my studies first —till something really worthwhile comes along in showbiz. This may be soon—though not so soon. But—be that as it may—I try to be ready for any 'emergency.' "

Evelyn is a big girl now.

HELEN HULL JACOBS

She won the United States Women's Singles Championship in 1932, 1933, 1934, and 1935, thereby becoming the first woman to win the title four years successively. She also held the United States Women's Doubles Championship in 1932, 1933, and 1934, including the 1934 Mixed Doubles with George Loft, now living in Chicago.

Helen Hull Jacobs was born in Globe, Arizona, on August 6, 1908. She attended the University of California at Berkeley from 1926 until 1929.

Helen's first title came in 1924 when she won the National Junior Tennis Championship, repeating the victory in 1925 as well. She was a member of the American Wightman Cup team from 1927 through 1938. In 1936 it was she who brought the Crown home to America for her Women's Singles victory at Wimbledon, England. Six different times Miss Jacobs was a finalist at the games in Wimbledon, spanning 1929 through 1938.

In 1942 Helen attended William and Mary College, entered the Waves in 1943 as a Lieutenant (j.g.), and served until 1945 as a public relations officer at the United States Training School in the Bronx, New York.

In 1947 she tore the Achilles tendon in one leg, and has not played tennis since. She was in a brace over seven months because of the accident, and was advised never to attempt the strenuous game again.

Recalled to active duty in 1949, Helen served as the Public Relations Officer at the Naval Gun Factory in Washington, D.C. In 1952 she was assigned as Administrative Assistant and Public Relations Officer to the

In 1934, the year she won both the singles and doubles. *U.S. Lawn Tennis Association*

A recent pose—she has not played for many years. *Asbury Park Press*, N.J.

Naval Station in Dalgren, Virginia, and in 1953 became Officer in Charge of Enlisted Personnel (inactive) in New York City. Since 1954 Miss Jacobs has been on inactive status with the role of Commander U.S.N. (ret.).

After leaving the service Helen lived and worked in New York City. She designed sports clothes for women, and was from 1961 until recently Senior Editor of the Grolier Company, working on their Book of Knowledge.

Of the famous feuds between the two Queens of Tennis, Helen Hull Jacobs and Helen Wills Moody, Miss Jacobs said recently, "We didn't know how it started and we didn't know how to stop it. She was never anything but extremely pleasant whenever we met." They have not seen each other since 1938.

She is currently working on her nineteenth book, her first an autobiography, *Beyond the Game,* written in 1936. Some of her other books are *Storm Against the Wind* and several about a character named Judy: *Laurel for Judy, Judy, Tennis Ace,* and also *Young Sportsman's Guide to Tennis.* Miss Jacobs has written a number of articles which have appeared in national magazines.

Helen Jacobs is a joiner. She is a member of Kappa Alpha Theta, the San Francisco Press Club, the Berkeley Tennis Club, the All England Lawn Tennis and Croquet Club, and the English Speaking Union in London. She has never married, and lives in a midtown Manhattan residential hotel.

CARL HUBBELL

Carl was born in Carthage, Missouri, in 1903 and came to professional baseball playing with the Beaumont team in the Texas League, until 1928, when he moved up to the big leagues—and the New York Giants.

There the lean left-handed pitcher had his finest hour in a game that added nothing to the Giants' race for the pennant or winning the World Series—the 1933 season had already seen "The Meal Ticket," as Hubbell was called, pace the Giants to the National League flag with 23 victories, and the subsequent World Series began with the hero pitching two more victories (20 innings without allowing an earned run), enabling the Giants to crush the Washington Senators in five games.

It was only natural, then, for the stylish screwball artist to be the starting pitcher for the National League in the 1934 All-Star game—the vehicle for that finest hour. The American League lineup featured the five most feared batsmen in many a day—Babe Ruth, Lou Gehrig, Jimmy Foxx, Al Simmons, and Joe Cronin. They came up to the plate in that order. They went down in that order—all on strikes. Baseball had never seen a pitching exhibition like it.

Hubbell had great moments, however, before and after that game: in 1929 he pitched a no-hit game, which ended in a score of 11–0 against the Pittsburgh Pirates, pitched a straight 46⅓ scoreless innings in 1933, and was voted both in 1933 and 1936 the most valuable player in the National

League by the Baseball Writers Association. A statistical example of three great years is:

Earned Run Leader	Innings Pitched	Earned Run Average
1933	309	1.66
1934	313	2.30
1936	303	2.31

Other great moments were five straight seasons (1933–1937) when he won 21 or more games, winning 16 in a row in 1936—24 straight if you count the 8 he won at the start of the 1937 season, and in 1936 and 1937 he was the National League pitching champion, in 1936 winning 26 and losing 6, in 1937 winning 22 and losing 8. In 1940 he pitched a one-hitter in which he faced the minimum 27 batters.

In 16 major league seasons (1928–1943), all with the New York Giants, Hubbell racked up 253 victories and a lifetime earned-run average of 2.98 and a career average of less than 2 walks per game.

Had Carl not overworked his arm he would probably have gone on for several more seasons. He retired from playing in 1943, which enabled him to see more of his two sons, Carl Owen, Jr., and James. He has remained with the Giants ever since in the capacity of director of the team's San Francisco farm system, in the meantime, in 1947, being named to the Baseball Hall of Fame. Carl lives in Burlingame, California, and spends his leisure time playing golf.

After pitching a 19-inning, 1–0 victory against the St. Louis Cardinals, 1933 *(far left)*.

Working out of an office now, in Candlestick Park, San Francisco.